ESSENTIAL
JUDAISM
IN A
NUTSHELL

ESSENTIAL JUDAISM IN A NUTSHELL

❊

RABBI
RONALD H. ISAACS

KTAV Publishing House, Inc.
Jersey City, New Jersey

Library of Congress Cataloging-in-Publication Data

Isaacs, Ronald H.
  Essential Judaism in a nutshell / Ronald Isaacs.
     p. cm.
  ISBN 0-88125-837-7
  1. Judaism. I. Title.
  BM45.I75 2004
  296--dc22

                                          2004003713

Published by
KTAV Publishing House, Inc.
930 Newark Avenue
Jersey City, NJ 07306
Email: info@ktav.com
www.ktav.com
(201) 963-9524
Fax (201) 963-0102

CONTENTS

INTRODUCTION

Judaism is a religion of about fourteen million Jews, who live in all parts of the world. It is the oldest religion of the Western world, and the first to teach monotheism or belief in one God. Judaism is founded on the laws and teachings of the Hebrew Bible, as well as rabbinic writings, including the Talmud and the various Jewish codes of law.

To be a Jew is to be immersed in a body of knowledge that represents the thoughts and behaviors of Jewish life. Jewish knowledge continues to evolve, ever since it was revealed to the Jewish people on that fiery mountaintop in Sinai almost 3500 years ago. Throughout Jewish history, Jews have communicated with one another through Jewish texts and contexts. Thus, one needs basic Jewish knowledge and vocabulary in order to function in and have an appreciation of Jewish life.

Essential Judaism in a Nutshell is intended as an introductory volume toward that quest. It is, as its title suggests, a presentation of basic Judaism in a nutshell. In the book you will find words, terms, dates, and key vocabulary and concepts related to the Jewish religion, its people, holidays and religion that are essential to an understanding of Judaism as both a religion and a way of life. In no way is this compilation to be considered definitive and exhaustive. Rather, it is meant to serve as a handy guide of reference information. The book is thus useful both to Jews and non-Jews who are interested in learning more about the Jewish people and their way of life in a user-friendly way.

PRINCIPAL TENETS OF JUDAISM

The Talmud (Pirke Avot 1:2) speaks of three central principles in life: Torah (learning), service of God, and the performance of good deeds. Thus love of learning and the importance of an education, worshipping God out of love, and righteous giving are three basic Jewish teachings.

Love of learning has always dominated Jewish faith. As long ago as the first century of the common era, Jews had a system of compulsory education.

The second basic teaching of Jewish faith is service of God. Judaism holds that people can most genuinely worship God by imitating those qualities that are godly: as God is merciful, so Jews must be compassionate; as God is just and righteous, so Jews must deal justly with our fellow human beings; as God is slow to anger, so Jews must be tolerant in their judgment. At the core of Judaism is ethics and a person's decency. In the Bible, the root "tzedek", meaning righteousness, occurs over five hundred times, including all of its inflections. The Jewish ideal is not only for a person to behave ethically, but to have an ethical character. A good person cannot and must not ever rest, but always strive to do better and be proactive and to make further progress toward the ultimate goal—the perfection of the world and getting closer to God.

A third tenet of Judaism is "tzedakah"—"righteous giving." Philanthropy for the pious Jew knows no racial or religious boundaries. Jews are required to feed the poor of the non Jewish world as well as that of the Jewish world. And no one, not even a poor person, is exempt from the practice of "tzedakah".

In the ancient academies it was common for the scholars to compete with one another in trying to devise the simplest formula for Judaism to be followed as a way of life. Here are several of the rabbinic formulae based on biblical verses and recorded in the Talmud Makkot 23a–24b.

1. The centrality of ethical behavior: "God has told you, O man, what is good, and what God requires of you: only to do justice, love goodness, and to walk humbly with your God. (Micah 6:8)

2. Rabbi Akiba said: "Love your neighbor as yourself" [Leviticus 19:18]—this is the major principle of the Torah. (Jerusalem Talmud Nedarim 9:4)

3. King David summed up the 613 commandments in these 11 ethical principles [Psalm 15:1–5]
i. One who lives without blame.
ii. One who does righteous acts
iii. One who speaks the truth in one's heart.
iv. One whose tongue speaks no deceit
v. One who has not done harm to his fellow
vi. One who has not borne reproach for his acts toward his neighbor
vii One for whom a contemptible person is abhorrent
viii. One who honors those who fear the Lord

ix. One who stands by his oath even when it is to his disadvantage

x. One who has never lent money for interest

xi. One who has not accepted a bribe against the innocent.(Talmud Makkot 23b)

4. The Prophet Habakkuk summed up the 613 commandments in this one principle: "The righteous shall live according to his faith." [2:4] (Talmud Makkot 24a)

5. Isaiah sums up the 613 commandments in these two principles:

i. Do justice

ii. Carry out acts of righteousness

Here is one final statement of Judaism's essence:

The following are the activities for which a person is rewarded in this world, and again in the World-To-Come: honoring one's parents, deeds of kindness, and making peace between a person and his neighbor. The study of the Torah, however, is as important as all of them together. (Mishna Peah 1:1)

The most famous creed of faith in all of Judaism is Maimonides' Thirteen Principles of Faith. Following are his famous thirteen principles:

1. I believe with perfect faith that the Creator, blessed be Your name, is the Author and Guide of everything that has been created, and that God alone has made, does make and will make all things.

2. I believe with perfect faith that the Creator, blessed be Your name, is a Unity, and that there is no unity in any manner like unto You, and that You alone are our God, who was, is and will be.

3. I believe with perfect faith that the Creator, blessed be Your name, is not a body, and that You are free from all the accidents of matter, and that You have not any form whatsoever.

7

4. I belief with perfect faith that the Creator, blessed be Your name, is the first and the last.

5. I believe with perfect faith that to the Creator, blessed be Your name, and to You alone, it is right to pray, and that it is not right to pray to any being besides You.

6. I believe with perfect faith that all the words of the prophets are true.

7. I believe with perfect faith that the prophecy of Moses our teacher was true, and that he was the chief of the prophets, both of those that preceded and of those that followed him.

8. I believe with perfect faith that the whole Torah, now in our possession, is the same that was given to Moses our teacher, peace be unto him.

9. I believe with perfect faith that this Torah will not be changed, and that there will

never be any other law from the Creator, blessed be Your name.

10. I believe with perfect faith that the Creator, blessed be Your name, knows every deed of the human race, and all of their thoughts.

11. I believe with perfect faith that the Creator, blessed be Your name, rewards those that keep Your mitzvot and punishes those who transgress them.

12. I believe with perfect faith in the coming of the Messiah, and though the Messiah tarry, I will wait daily for his coming.

13. I believe with perfect faith that there will be a resurrection of the dead at the time when it shall please the Creator.

JEWISH CALENDAR

Unlike the secular Gregorian calendar which is solar, the Jewish calendar is both lunar and solar. The months are fixed by the moon's movements around the earth, the years by the earth's revolution around the sun. Originally the Jewish calendar was purely lunar, with the year ending after twelve months had elapsed. But since lunar months are shorter than solar ones, the seasons soon began to shift. Spring, for instance, occurred a few days earlier every year, and the Jewish holidays began not to fall in their specified seasons. To prevent this problem, a system of coordinating the lunar year with the solar year was devised, including the insertion of a "leap month" every few years.

In biblical times, the first month of the Hebrew calendar was Nisan. On the fifteenth of this month, the Israelites achieved freedom from Egyptian slavery. The return from the Babylonian Exile, however, occurred in the fall, and that is why Rosh Hashanah, the festival of the New Year, is celebrated on the first day of the autumn month of Tishri.

There are twelve months in the Hebrew calendar. Based on the moon's cycle around the earth, each of them has either 29 or 30 days, thus making the lunar year 354 days long. By contrast, a solar year is 365 days. To make up for the difference and keep the lunar year cycle on track with the solar year, an extra month (Adar II) is added to the Jewish year approximately once every three years.

Here are the names of the months of the Hebrew calendar:
1. Nisan
2. Iyar
3. Sivan
4. Tammuz
5. Av
6. Elul
7. Tishri
8. Heshvan
9. Kislev

10. Tevet
11. Shevat
12. Adar
13. Adar II (only in a leap year)

The Jewish calendar numbers the years from the date of the world's creation as determined by Jewish tradition. The book you are now reading was first published in 5764 (2004); in other words, 5764 years after the beginning of the world—or symbolically, since the beginning of consciously recorded time. The secular calendar, in contrast, counts years from the birth of Jesus, using the abbreviation A.D. (anno domini, meaning "in the year of our Lord"). Dates before the birth of Jesus are followed by the abbreviation B.C. ("before Christ"). Thus A.D. 2004 means 2004 years after the birth of Jesus. For Jews and others sensitive to Jewish tradition, it is customary when citing dates in the civil calendar to use the abbreviation C.E. ("common era") instead of A.D., and B.C.E. ("before the common era") instead of B.C.

THE JEWISH HOLIDAYS

Judaism is primarily a home celebration, with a variety of Jewish holidays through the year. In a nutshell, here is a summary of the dates (or the beginnings) of the Jewish festivals:

14 Nisan	Pesach (Passover)
27 Nisan	Yom HaShoah (Holocaust Remembrance Day)
4 Iyar	Yom Hazikaron (Israel Remembrance Day)
5 Iyar	Yom Ha'atzma'ut (Israel Independence Day)
28 Iyar	Yom Yerushalayim (Jerusalem Day)
6 Sivan	Shavuot (Feast of Weeks)
9 Av	Tisha B'Av (Fast of the 9th of Av)
1 Tishri	Rosh Hashanah (New Year)
10 Tishri	Yom Kippur (Day of Atonement)
14 Tishri	Sukkot (Festival of Booths)
22 Tishri	Shemini Atzeret

23 Tishri	Simchat Torah
25 Kislev	Hanukkah
15 Shevat	Tu Beshevat (Jewish Arbor Day)
14 Adar	Purim (Festival of Lots)

JEWISH HOLIDAYS IN A NUTSHELL

Shabbat (Sabbath)

Date: Seventh day of every week
Duration: One day (from sundown on Friday until approximately 25 hours later on Saturday night)
Name of Holiday: Day of Rest (Yom Menuha)
Source: God blessed the seventh day and declared it holy, because on it God ceased from all the work of creation. (Genesis 2:3)
General Theme: Commemorates the creation of the world. It is a day devoted to prayer, study, rest, relaxation, spirituality and enjoyment.
Personal Theme: An occasion to cease from daily work and relax, proclaiming God the Sovereign of the world.
Traditional Food: Braided loaves of bread (hallot), gefilte fish, wine and chicken.

Customs: Preparation for the Sabbath would include house cleaning, personal cleanliness and giving money to charity. Two candles are lit just before sunset and the appropriate blessing is recited. (see pg. 152) Traditionally a festive meal is served after the Friday evening service. At the synagogue service on Saturday morning a "sidrah" (selection) from the Torah (Scroll of the Five Books of Moses) is read, followed by the reading of a prophetic portion known as the "Haftarah." The Sabbath afternoon may included taking a nap, reading, studying, and the like. The Saturday evening service concludes with the ceremony of separation known as Havdalah. Its ceremonial objects include a cup filled with wine (sanctifying reentry into the secular world), a spice box (to help the memory of the holy Sabbath linger) and a braided multi-wick candle (reminder that light was the first of God's creations after the heaven and earth)

Rosh HaShanah (New Year)

Date: First two days of Tishri
Duration: Two days for Conservative, Reconstructionist and Orthodox Jews and for Jews in Israel. One day for Reform Jews.
Names of Holiday: Yom Teruah (day of blowing the ram's horn), Yom HaZikaron (day of remembrance) and Yom Hadin (day of judgment)
Source: In the seventh month, on the first day of the month, you shall observe a complete rest, a sacred occasion commemorated with loud blasts. (Leviticus 23:24)
General Theme: God judges people for the coming year and symbolically weighs their acts. Rosh Hashanah also commemorates the birthday of the world.
Personal Theme: Renewal, admitting mistakes and asking for forgiveness.
Foods: Round hallot, suggesting a royal crown (i.e. God's sovereignty), apples dipped in honey (symbolizing a sweet year)
Customs: A festive meal is serve in which

the blessing over the wine is recited and apples are dipped in honey. During synagogue services the rabbi and the cantor (and congregants who follow this custom) wear a white robe, called a "kittel", symbolizing purity and renewal. When greeting people, one customarily uses the Hebrew phrase "l'shanah tova tikatevu" ("May you be inscribed for a good year") The shofar (ram's horn) is sounded during services (except when Rosh Hashanah falls on the Sabbath), intended to awaken people to doing penitence. On the first day of Rosh Hashanah in the afternoon (the second day if Rosh Hashanah falls on the Sabbath), Jews gather at a nearby stream or river to symbolically cast away their transgressions in a ceremony called"Tashlich." They throw bread crumbs (symbolizing their misdeeds) into the river.

Yom Kippur
(Day of Atonement)

Date: Tenth of Tishri

Duration: One day for Jews of all denominations and in all places.

Name of Holiday: Sabbath of Sabbaths (Shabbat Shabbaton)

Source: The tenth day of this seventh month is the Day of Atonement. It shall be a sacred occasion for you: you shall practice self-denial...(Leviticus 23:27)

General Theme: Confessing our sins and asking for forgiveness, Jews pray that they will be written in God's Book of Life.

Personal Theme: Atonement, integrity and renewal.

Customs: Adult Jews fast throughout the entirety of the Day of Atonement. Abstinence also includes bathing, and not using leather shoes (out of compassion for animals) and not adorning oneself with cosmetics. Just before leaving for services on the eve of the Day of Atonement, the custom is to light a yahrzeit candle as a memorial to the deceased members of the family. The greeting at the end of Yom Kippur is "G'mar hatimah tovah"—"may you be sealed in the Book of Life for a good verdict."

Sukkot (Festival of Booths)

Date: Begins on the fifteenth of Tishri.
Duration: Eight days for Conservative, Reconstructionist and Orthodox Jews. Seven days for Reform and Jews in Israel.
Names of Holiday: Festival of Ingathering (Hag He-asif); The Festival (He-Hag); Day of Rejoicing (Zeman Simhateinu); Harvest Festival (Hag Ha-katzir)
Source: On the fifteenth of the seventh month there shall be a Feast of Booths to God, (to last) seven days. On the first day you shall take the produce of hadar trees, branches of palm trees, boughs of leafy trees and willows of the brook, and you shall rejoice before God seven days. You

shall live in booths seven days. (Leviticus 23:24,40,42)

General Theme: Sukkot marks the end of the fall harvest season, when the Israelites brought their first fruits to the Temple as a thanksgiving offering. It also commemorates the Israelites' forty years of wandering in the desert, in which they built fragile huts to protect themselves from the elements. Jews are commanded to spend time in their sukkot (huts) as a way of reminding themselves of the fragility of life.

The Bible commands the use of so-called "four species" on Sukkot. These consist of the etrog (citron), the lulav (palm branch), and attached to the lulav two sets of leaves—hadassim—myrtle, which are short and round, and aravot, (willows, which are long and narrow) Various explanations are given for the four species, including one in which the etrog symbolizes the heart, the lulav the spine, the myrtle the eyes and the willow the lips and mouth. Thus the four species indicate that Jews are to serve God with every part of their being.

Personal Theme: A Thanksgiving festival with many similarities to the American Thanksgiving holiday.

Traditional Food: Stuffed cabbage and kreplach (fried pockets of dough) containing meat, fruit and fall harvest vegetables.

Customs: The holiday is ushered in with the festival blessing. The blessing over the wine and challah is chanted in the sukkah, which is erected for the holiday. During synagogue morning services Hallel Psalms of praise are chanted and the lulav and etrog are waved in a prescribed pattern of movement. The lulav and etrog are also carried in a procession during morning service while Hoshannot prayers for redemption are recited. Meals are customarily served in the sukkah throughout the festival.

The seventh day of Sukkot is called Hoshana Rabbah ("The Great Help). On that day the cantor dons a white gown. It is said that on this day God's judgment, sealed on the Day of Atonement, receives final confirmation. Seven circuits are made around the sanctuary with the Torah carrier in the lead, followed by worshippers carrying their lulav and etrog. At the service's end, a specially prepared bunch of willow leaves (hoshannot) are taken and struck against a chair or table by the worshippers. Just as a tree, after losing its leaves, renews its life through rain and warmth, so the Jewish people can gain fresh strength for life's struggles by renewed faith in God. The separation of the leaves from the twigs also symbolizes the separation of sin from their lives.

The Book of Ecclesiastes is also read during the Festival of Sukkot. Finally, the greeting during Sukkot is "hag samei'ach" (happy holiday) or "moadim lesimha" (may your festival be happy")

Shemini Atzeret and Simhat Torah

Date: Twenty-second and twenty-third of Tishri.

Duration: Two days for Conservative, Reconstructionist and Orthodox Jews. One day for Reform Jews and Jews living in Israel.

Source: On the eighth day you shall observe a sacred occasion...it is a solemn gathering: you shall not work at your occupations. (Leviticus 23:36)

General Theme: Shemini Atzeret is an extension of the Festival of Sukkot, an eighth day that allows for festivities to linger. The ninth day (Simhat Torah) is the conclusion of the reading of Deuteronomy (that last book of the Five Books of Moses) and the reading anew of the beginning of the Torah with the story of creation in the Book of Genesis.

Personal Theme: A new beginning in anticipation of an improved year.

Customs: Candles are lit on both the evening of Shemini Atzeret and Simhat Torah. Festive meals with blessings over wine and challah are recited as well. On Shemini Atzeret, the Yizkor Memorial prayers for the departed are recited as well as the special prayer "Tefillat Geshem" for rain in Israel. On Simchat Torah there is much merry making, dancing and singing. Children often carry small Torah scrolls, banners and flags. In addition, it is customary to call every adult member to the Torah for an aliyah. Sometimes adults are called up collectively to say the Torah blessings, standing under a large prayer shawl. (tallit) Children too are given the opportunity to recite the Torah blessings while standing under a tallit.

Hanukkah

Date: Begins on the twenty fifth of Kislev
Duration: Eight Days
Name: Festival of Lights (Hag Ha-urim)
Source: They purified the Temple...rebuilt the Sanctuary and restored its interior and courts...Then on the twenty fifth of the month of Kislev...it was rededicated with hymns of thanksgiving. (I Maccabees 4:39–59)

General Theme: Hanukkah marks the first time in recorded history that a war was fought to win freedom of religion. Antiochus, the Syrian King suffered a stunning defeat at the hand of the Maccabees, who not only defeated him but rededicated the Temple in Jerusalem. According to legend, there was just one small cruse of pure oil when they entered the Temple, but through a miracle it burned for eight days. Thus candles are burnt each successive night of the eight nights of Hanukkah, placed in a candleholder called a "hanukkiah."

Personal Theme: Religious freedom and dedication

Traditional Foods: Foods fried in oil such as potato pancakes (latkes) or jelly donuts (called *sufganiyot*) which are popular in Israel.

Customs: Each night of Hanukkah the hanukkiah is lit and the appropriate blessings recited. (see pg. 153 for the Hanukkah blessings) The hymn "Rock of Ages" (Ma'oz Tzur) is also often chanted. In the synagogue the special Hallel Psalms of praise are chanted throughout the holiday. At home, Hanukkah games are often played. The most popular one is the dreidel game, a four-sided spinning top. Each side is marked with a Hebrew letter, nun, gimel, hay shin, which together stand for the words "Nes gadol hayah sham"—" a great miracle happened there") Players take turns spinning the dreidel. For "nun", you get nothing; for "gimel", you take all; for "hay" you take half, and if it falls on "shin", the player must add to the pot. Sharing and exchanging gifts, including Hanukkah "gelt" (i.e. money) is also a popular Hanukkah pastime.

A popular Hanukkah activity is affixing a new "mezuzah" to a doorpost of one's home that has not yet received one. This is a way of spiritually dedicating a room, and fits well with the meaning of the word Hanukkah—namely "dedication."

Tu Beshevat
(Jewish Arbor Day)

Date: Fifteenth of Shevat
Duration: One day
Name of Holiday: New Year for Trees ("Rosh Hashanah L'ilanot")
Source: Mentioned in the mishnah (Rosh Hashanah 1:1)
Theme: Tu Beshevat commemorates the beginning of the spring season in Israel, when the trees begin to blossom. In Israel children and adults plants trees. In the Diaspora it is customary to purchase Jewish National Fund (i.e. the official organization responsible for planting trees in Israel) certificates.
Traditional Foods: Fruits and vegetables are customarily eaten on Tu Beshevat. These may include Israeli fruits mentioned in the Bible, including grapes, pomegranates, figs, dates, olives and "bokser" (St. John's Bread), the fruit of the carob tree.
Customs: 1. Some synagogues and families hold a Tu Beshevat seder using four cups of

wine (one white, symbol of winter; the second light red, symbol of spring; the third, deep red, the symbol of summer and the fourth, red mixed with white, symbol of fall). A special Tu Beshevat Haggadah is often used to recite blessings over the various fruits.

2. In Israel children plant saplings in the Jewish National Fund forests. In Western countries the custom is to purchase tree certificates in honor and memory of friends and relatives.

Purim

Date: Fourteenth of Adar
Duration: One day
Source: For that reason these days were named Purim, after "pur," (i.e. "lot") {Esther 9:26}
General Theme: Purim commemorates an amazing escape from persecution about 2400 years ago in Persia. Mordecai, a Jewish leader refused to bow down to

Haman, vizier of King Ahasuerus. The angry Haman obtained permission to kill all Persian Jews and drew lots ("purim" in Hebrew) to determine the day of the massacre. Through the intervention of Mordecai's niece Queen Esther, the Jews were saved.

Personal Theme: Giving to the poor and sharing food with one's friends.

Traditional Food: "Hamantaschen" (triangular pastry often filled with prunes, poppy seeds, and the like) The shape of this pastry was said to be reminiscent of Haman's three- cornered hat.

Customs: The day before Purim is "Ta'anit Esther"—Esther's fast. Some Jews fast thus honoring Esther who abstained from food for three days before petitioning King Ahasuerus on behalf of her people. The Scroll of Esther ("Megillat Esther") is publicly chanted in the synagogue both in the evening and morning of Purim day. Worshippers are encouraged to masquerade in costume and to use noisemakers (called "greggars" or "ra'ashaneem" in

Hebrew) to drown out Haman's name each time that it is read. Purim carnivals are popular during the festival, as is a festive Purim meal (called the "Purim seudah"), customarily served in the late afternoon. Merrymaking and jesting are popular activities during this festival meal.

Sending food baskets ("shalach manot") to family and friends and making charitable contributions to the poor ("matanot le'evyoneem") are two important religious obligations.

Pesah (Passover)

Date: Begins the fourteenth of Nisan.
Duration: Eight days for Conservative, Reconstructionist and Orthodox Jews. Seven days for Reform and Jews living in Israel.
Names of holiday: 1. Feast of Unleavened Bread. (Hag HaMatzot)
2. Festival of Spring (Hag He'Aviv)
3. Passover (Pesach) This name is derived

from the Hebrew word "pasach" ("passed over"). The Torah says that the Angel of the Lord "passed over" the Israelite homes while smiting the firstborn Egyptians (Exodus 12:27)

Source: In the first month, on the fourteenth of the month, at twilight, there shall be a Passover offering to God...You shall eat unleavened bread for seven days. (Leviticus 23:5)

General Theme: Passover commemorates the exodus of the Israelites from Egypt. During their hasty departure, the Israelites did not have time to let their bread dough rise. The result was "matzah"—unleavened bread, which Jews eat today on Passover as a reminder of their Egyptian bondage. Passover is also an agricultural holiday heralding the arrival of spring and the beginning of the spring harvest.

Personal Theme: Religious Freedom.

Traditional Foods: 1. During the Passover seder meal, the following special foods are placed on the Seder plate:

Haroset: Mixture of chopped nuts, apples, and wine recalling the mortar used by the Israelite slaves to make bricks for the pyramids.

Roasted Bone. ("Zeroa"): Represents the paschal lamb which was sacrificed by our ancestors.

Roasted Egg ("beitzah") Symbolizes both the sacrifice made by everyone in the Temple on each holiday and the mourning of the destruction of the Temple.

Bitter Herbs ("Maror") Pure horseradish, symbolizing the bitterness of slavery.

Parsley. ("karpas"): Symbolizing spring, it is dipped into salt water, symbolizing the tears of misery that were shed by the Israelite slaves.

2. Food that is leavened ("hametz") may not be eaten on Passover. This includes foods made from wheat, rye, barley, oats, and spelt.

Customs: 1. Before the festival begins, it is customary to search for any leftover "hametz" in a ceremony called "bedikat hametz"—"searching for leaven." The ceremony is conducted using a wooden spoon as a dustpan, a candle for light and a feather for a broom. On the morning of the eve of Passover, the "hametz" that was gathered the night before is burned.

2. A Passover Seder is conducted on the first two nights of Passover (one night for Reform Jews) The text used during the meal is the "Haggadah"

3. Historically, "wheat money" ("ma'ot hittin") was given to the poor. Today the custom is to make a charitable contribution.

4. Beginning on the second night of Passover, Jews count the "omer". The "omer" (literally "sheaf" of barley), refers to an offering from the new barley crop which was brought to the Temple on the eve of the second day of Passover. Omer has come to be associated as the period between Passover and Shavuot of 49 days. By counting the days of this period (called "sefirat ha'omer"), Jews heighten their anticipation to the long awaited festival of Shavuot, cel-

ebrating God's revelation atop of Mount Sinai.

5. On the last day of Passover it is customary to light a yahrzeit candle in one's home in memory of the departed. The following morning during services the Yizkor memorial service is recited in honor of the dead.

6. Some synagogues follow the custom of reading selections from the biblical book the Song of Songs. Rabbinic tradition interprets the book as a love song between God and the people of Israel.

Shavuot (Festival of Weeks)

Date: Begins the sixth of Sivan
Duration: Two days for Conservative, Reconstructionist and Orthodox Jews. One day for Reform Jews and Jews living in Israel.
Names of holiday: 1. Season of the Giving of Our Torah ("Z'man Matan Torateinu)

2. Holiday of First Fruits (Hag HaBikkurim)

Source: You must count until the day after the seventh week—fifty days; then you shall bring an offering of new grain to God. (Leviticus 23:16)

General Theme: The festival commemorates the Israelites' receiving the Torah at Mount Sinai. As one of the three pilgrimage festivals, Israelites would bring an offering of the first fruits ("bikkurim") to the Temple in Jerusalem. Thus, Shavuot has also come to be known as the spring harvest festival of first fruits.

Personal Theme: Acceptance of religious obligations ("mitzvot") and reaffirmation of our covenant with God.

Traditional Food: Blintzes, cheesecake and other dairy foods. The passage "honey and milk shall be under your tongue" (Song of Songs 4:1) was rabbinically understood to imply that the words of the Torah shall be pleasant to our ears and heart as milk and honey are to our tongue.

Customs: 1. Lighting holiday candles and making kiddush, to usher in the festival and having a festive meal.

2. Spend time on Shavuot night studying Jewish texts. This special gathering is called "tikkun leil shavuot."

3. Synagogues are decorated with greenery and flowers reflecting the spring harvest.

4. A yahrzeit memorial candle is kindled in the home in memory of one's deceased loved ones. At Shacharit morning services there is a Yizkor Memorial service.

5. Many synagogues hold a Confirmation service on Shavuot for their High school students. In the service the Hebrew High School students confirm their love for God, Torah and Israel.

6. On Shavuot the Book of Ruth is read. Ruth, a Moabite woman came to embrace the religion of Israel, and her story takes place at the time of the spring harvest. In addition, tradition records that King David was descended from Ruth who was born and died on Shavuot.

Tisha B'Av (Ninth of Av)

Date: Ninth of Av
Duration: One day
Theme: Tisha B'av commemorates the destruction of the First and Second Temples in Jerusalem.
Customs: 1. The fast of Tisha B'Av begins at the end of the evening meal. On the night of Tisha B'av worshippers gather in the synagogue and often sit on low benches or on the floor. Using candle light, the Book of Lamentations ("Eicha") is chanted. 2. Eating, drinking, bathing and conjugal relations are forbidden during the commemoration of the Ninth of Av.

Yom HaShoah (Holocaust Memorial Day)

Date: Twenty-seventh of Nisan.
Duration: One day.
Theme: A day to recall the six million Jews

of Europe who were murdered during the Second World War by the Nazis.

Customs: 1. A synagogue or community wide memorial service is held in honor of the dead. Holocaust survivors and their children often speak at the service, and a six branched candelabrum is lit in memory of the six million that perished.

Yom HaZikaron (Remembrance Day)

Date: Fourth of Iyar
Duration: One day.
Theme: An Israeli memorial day observed for soldiers killed in defense of Israel from the War of Independence (1948) through the present day. It is observed with solemn civil, military and religious ceremonies throughout Israel.
Customs: 1. Memorial candles are lit in army camps, schools, synagogues, and flags are flown at half-mast.

2. In the morning in Israel sirens mark a two minute silence throughout the country which brings all activity to a standstill.

Yom Ha-Atzma'ut
(Israel Independence Day)

Date: Fifth of Iyar
Duration: One day
Theme: Commemorates the establishment of the State of Israel on May 14, 1948, corresponding to the fifth of Iyar, 5708.
Traditional Foods: Israel foods, such as pita, falafel and humus.
Customs: Public gatherings and celebrations take place, including Israeli day parades.

Lag B'Omer
(Thirty-third Day of the Omer)

Date: Eighteenth of Iyar.
Duration: One day
Theme: The days between Passover and Shavuot are a solemn period recalling the suffering which the Jews endured under Roman persecution. Lag B'Omer breaks the series of solemn days. According to Jewish folklore, this is because Bar Kochba won a great victory over the Romans on the thirty third day of the omer. Another tradition relates that on this day a plague that was raging among Rabbi Akiba's students suddenly stopped.
Name: Scholar's holiday.
Customs: 1. Weddings are often held on Lag B'Omer, because of the joyousness of the day.
2. Picnics, outings, games , sporting events and bonfires are popular ways of celebrating.

3. Traditional Jews often give their children their first haircut on Lag B'Omer.

SIX YEAR CALENDAR OF JEWISH HOLIDAYS

Year	Passover	Shavuot	Yom Kippur	Shemini Atzeret
2005	April 24	June 14 (*13)	Oct 13	Oct 25 (*24)
2006	April 20	June 3 (*2)	Oct 2	Oct. 14 (*13)
2007	April 3	May 24 (*23)	Sept 22	Oct 4 (*3)
2008	April 20	June 10 (*9)	Oct. 9	Oct. 21 (*20)
2009	April 9	May 30 (*29)	Sept. 28	Oct. 10 (*9)
2010	March 30	May 20 (*19)	Sept. 18	Sept. 30 (*29)

Note: (*) signifies Reform observance

JEWISH TEXTS IN A NUTSHELL

Jews throughout the ages have been known as the People of the Book. Following are the important books of the Jewish people and a brief description of their contents.

Tanakh: The Hebrew Bible

1. **The Tanakh**: The Tanakh is an acronym for the three categories of books that make up the thirty-nine books of the Hebrew Bible: Torah, Nevi'im (Prophets) and Ketuvim. (Writings) Following are all of the books that make up the Jewish Bible:

Books of the Torah: The Torah is the Five Books of Moses, which are:
i. Genesis (in Hebrew, "Beresheet"): Tells the story of creation and the story of the three patriarchs Abraham, Isaac and Jacob

and the four matriarchs—Sarah, Rachel, Rebekah and Leah.

ii. Exodus (in Hebrew, "Shemot") Tells the story of Egyptian oppression of the Israelites, the appearance of Moses, the Ten Plagues, the exodus from Egypt and the giving of the Ten Commandments at Mount Sinai.

iii. Leviticus (in Hebrew, "Vayikra"): Contains a manual for the Levites, the priestly ritual of sacrifices, the Holiness Code, rules regarding charity, marriage and laws governing many other aspects of life.

iv. Numbers (in Hebrew, "Bamidbar"): Tells the story of the Israelites during their wandering in the desert from the second to the fortieth year of the exodus.

v. Deuteronomy: (In Hebrew, "Devarim"): This book as been identified as the lost book found in the Temple during the reign of King Josiah. Many of the ethical ideas found in the earlier books of the Five Books of Moses reach their loftiest form in the Book of Deuteronomy.

Books of the Prophets: Early Prophets

1. Joshua: Joshua was chosen to succeed Moses as Israel's leader. He led Israel across the Jordan, conquered the Jericho fortress and defeated the hostile Canaanite enemy.

2. Judges: This book spans the period from the death of Joshua to the time of Saul's coronation. The judges were called to leadership by the people and their battles eventually extended Israelite mastery of the land.

3. I Samuel: This book's contents include the priestly rule of the house of Eli, Samuel's anointing of Saul as Israel's first king and Saul's experiences and battles.
4. II Samuel: In this book David assumes the kingship of Hebron. The book features

David's preparation for rule over all Israel, his rule, wars, victories and conquests and rebellions against him

5. I Kings: The contents of this book includes David's last testament, the anointing of Solomon, the building of the Temple in Jerusalem, the division of the Kingdom of Israel after Solomon's death and the appearance and activity of Elijah.

6. II Kings: The contents includes the period of the two kingdoms of Israel, the activity of Elisha, the exile of Ephraim and the first exile of Judah under King Jehoiachin.

Later Prophets

1. Isaiah: Contains prophecies of Isaiah, the divine ethics, political counsel, moral preaching and words of comfort.

2. Jeremiah: Contains prophecies of Jeremiah, morality and prayer, injunctions

against the priests and false prophets, lamentations over the destruction of the Temple and words of comfort and consolation.

3. Ezekiel: Contains Ezekiels' visions of God, prophecies uttered in Babylon, the sins of Jerusalem and its ultimate destruction and consolation for the future.

Twelve Minor Prophets

1. Hosea: His book conceived of the relationship between God and Israel as an almost physical love.

2. Joel: In this book the Israelites are called to repent because the Day of Judgment is at hand.

3. Amos: In this book Amos warns the Israelites of the grave danger from Assyria. Righteousness for Amos was the most important moral attribute of the divine nature.

4. Obadiah: This one chapter book severely condemns Edom for having refused to assist Jerusalem in her hour of difficulty.

5. Jonah: This prophet is swallowed by a great fish after trying to flee from his mission to prophesy the destruction of Nineveh. After his wondrous deliverance he was obedient to his second commission from God. God ultimately spared the Ninevites when he saw its people repenting.

6. Micah: This prophet speaks for the people against the oppression of the ruling classes, being the first to threaten them with exile to Babylon.

7. Nahum: He foretold the fall of Nineveh.

8. Habakkuk: This book contains an outcry against the victory of the Chaldeans and the rule of iniquity in the world. It concludes with God's reply and a description of the Day of the Lord.

9. Zephaniah: His prophecies are mostly eschatological (i.e. looking into the far future). Described in the book is the Day of the Lord, when God will punish all the wicked and will be universally acknowledged.

10. Haggai: Haggai calls for the rebuilding of the Temple and foretells its glory.

11. Zechariah: His prophecies are concerned with contemporary events and foretell the ingathering of the exiles and the expansion of Jerusalem.

12. Malachi: Last of the biblical prophets, he protests against transgressions in matters of sacrifice and tithes and complains of mixed and broken marriages.

Writings

1. Psalms: Consists of 150 Psalms traditionally ascribed to King David, often called the Psalmist.

2. Proverbs: A collection of moral sayings.

3. Job: The theme of this book is divine justice and the problem of suffering of the righteous.

4. Song of Songs: Collection of poems about sexual love and courtship, symbolic of God's courtship with the children of Israel. Tradition ascribes its authorship to King Solomon.

5. Ruth: Ruth the Moabite woman accompanied her mother-in-law Naomi back to Bethlehem using the famous words "wherever you go, I will go..." In a sense, she becomes the first convert to Judaism.

6. Lamentations: Five chapters of elegies and mourning over the destruction by the Babylonians of Judea, Jerusalem and its Temple. According to tradition its author was Jeremiah.

7. Ecclesiastes ("Kohelet," in Hebrew).

Traditionally assigned to King Solomon, this book seeks to discern the purpose of human life with all its trials, but finds no spiritual support in either faith or intellect.

8. Esther: Central character in this biblical book, Esther was chosen by King Ahasuerus to be the queen in place of the deposed Vashti. She used her influence to save the Jewish people from the hand of Haman.

9. Daniel: The Prophet Daniel was taken captive to Babylon and trained for the king's service. When he interpreted some mysterious writing on a wall, symbolizing the downfall of the king, Daniel was cast into a den of lions. Miraculously though, he was saved from death.

10. Ezra: One of the leaders of the return from the Babylonian captivity, Ezra was a great teacher of the Law.

11. Nehemiah: Governor of Judea who

devoted himself to social reforms, including the stimulation of Sabbath observance, the cancellation of debts owed by the poor, and steps against mixed marriage. His work was decisive in the rebuilding of Judea.

12. I and II Chronicles: The last two books of the Hebrew Bible, they retell the history of the Jewish people from Creation to the close of the Babylonian exile. They concentrate on the history of the Kingdom of Judah and stress both Priestly duties and Temple ritual.

DATES OF IMPORTANT BIBLE EVENTS AND PERSONALITIES

(Note: All dates are B.C.E.)
(* Indicates approximate date)

Abraham	2000 (*2000–1700) Period of Patriarchs
Isaac	(*1700–1300) Period of Israelite tribes
Jacob	in Egypt
Joseph	1500
Moses	(*1300) Exodus of Israelites from Egypt
	(*1250) Entry in Canaan
	(*1225–1020) Period of Judges
Deborah	
Gideon	
Samson	
Samuel	(1020–1004) King Saul's reign
Saul	
Nathan	1000 (*998–965) King David's reign

Solomon	(*965–926) King Solomon's reign
	(*926) Hebrew kingdom divided; Jeroboam, King of Israel
Elijah	(*882–871) Omri, King of Israel
	(*871–852) Ahab, King of Israel
Elisha	
Amos	
Isaiah	
Hosea	
Micah	(721) Assyrian destruction of Israel
	(621) Book of Deuteronomy Discovered
Jeremiah	(598) First Babylonian invasion of Judah
	(589) Final Babylonian invasion of Judah
Ezekiel	
Second Isaiah	
	(*538) Edict of Cyrus of Persian, which permitted return of Israelite exiles
Ezra	500 (*450) Return of Ezra and Nehemiah

TALMUD:
BOOKS OF THE ORAL LAW

The Talmud is the rabbinic interpretation of the Bible, and the source for Jewish law. There is both a Babylonian and Palestinian Talmud, in which are collected the records of academic discussion and judicial administration of Jewish law by generations of scholars.

The following is a brief summary of the tractates of the Talmud and their contents:

First Order: "Zeraim"—Seeds: Deals with laws related to agriculture, contributions to the priests and Levites and laws concerning blessings. The tractates in this first order are as follows:

1. **Berachot (Blessings)**; First Talmudic tractate, dealing with laws of reciting the Shema, the Amidah, Grace after meals and various blessings.

2. **Pe'ah (Corner of Field)**: Deals with laws concerning harvest of corner of one's field to be given to the poor.

3. **Demai (Doubtfully Tithed)**: Deals with laws of doubtfully tithed produce.

4. **Kilayim (Mixtures)**: Deals with laws prohibiting grafting different species of plants, mixtures of cloth and cross-breeding of animals.

5. **Shevi'it (Sabbatical Year)**: Deals with laws of Sabbatical Year, when land is rested.

6. **Terumot (Contributions, the Priest's' Portion of the Harvest)**: Deals with laws of priests' portion of harvest.

7. **Ma'aserot (Tithes)**: Deals with laws of first and second tithe.

8. **Ma'aser Sheni (Second Tithe)**: Deals with laws of second tithe

9. **Hallah (Dough)**: Deals with laws of separating dough and giving it to priests.

10. **Orlah (Uncircumcised Fruit)**: Deals with prohibition of using fruits of trees during first three years after planting.

11. **Bikkurim (First Fruits)**: Deals with first fruit offerings at the Temple.

Second Order: Moed (Festivals): Deals with laws that apply to the Sabbath and festivals. The tractates in this second order are as follows:

1. **Shabbat (Sabbath)**; Contains most of laws of governing the Sabbath.
2. **Eruvin (Mergings)**: Deals with laws concerning boundaries within which one is allowed to carry and walk on the Sabbath.
3. **Pesachim (Passover)**: Deals with treatment of laws of Festival of Passover.
4. **Shekalim (Shekels)**: Deals with laws of the levy of the shekel to the Temple service.
5. **Yoma (Day of Atonement)**: Deals mainly with order of service in Temple on Yom Kippur.
6. **Sukkah (Booth)**: Deals with laws of a valid and invalid "sukkah".
7. **Betzah (Egg)**: Deals with laws that apply to all festivals and types of work prohibited on them.
8. **Rosh Hashanah (New Year)**: Deals with laws of fixing date of New Year, of calendar laws and laws regarding the ram's

horn and the prayer service on Rosh Hashanah.

9. **Ta'anit (Fast)**: Deals with public fast days and special prayers for rain.

10. **Megillah (Scroll)**: Deals with laws concerning the reading of the Scroll of Esther and commandments concerning Purim.

Third Order: Nashim (Women): Deals with pertaining to marriage. The following are the tractates in the third order of the Talmud:

1. **Yevamot (Sisters-in-law)**: Deals with laws of levirate marriage and halitzah (i.e. ceremony whereby a childless widow obtains release from the obligation to perform levirate marriage.

2. **Ketubot (Married deeds)**: Deals with laws of marriage deeds and obligations pertaining to husband and wife.

3. **Nedarim (Vows)**: Deals with all laws concerning vows.

4. **Nazir (Nazirite)**: Deals with the laws of the Nazirite.

5. **Sotah (Woman suspected of adultery)**: Deals with laws of a suspected adulterous woman and laws of priestly blessing and warfare.

6. **Gittin (Divorce)**: Deals with arrangements for writing a bill of divorce.

7. **Kiddushin**: Deals with various ways in which a woman may be betrothed and under what conditions.

Fourth Order: Nezikin (Damages): Deals with civil and criminal law, corporal and capital punishment the composition of Rabbinical Courts. The following tractates are in this fourth order:

1. **Bava Kamma (First Gate)**: Deals with civil law, especially laws relating to types of damage inflicted by one person on another.

2. **Bava Metziah (Middle Gate)**: Deals with disputes over financial matters and laws regarding lost property, deposits, loans, hiring labors, and laws of interest.

3. **Bava Batra (Last Gate)**; Deals with laws

of partnership, sales contracts for property and laws of inheritance.

4. **Sanhedrin: (Courts of Judges)**: Deals with laws of capital punishment.

5. **Makkot (Lashes)**: Deals with laws of corporal punishment and laws concerning false testimony.

6. **Shevuot (Oaths)**: Deals with types of oaths administered in the course of court hearings concerning monetary matters as well as various oaths instituted by the rabbis.

7. **Eduyyot (Testimonies)**: Deals with testimonies given by rabbis on a variety of legal subjects.

8. **Avodah Zarah (idolatry)**: Deals with idolatry and prohibited contacts between Jews and non-Jews.

9. **Avot (Fathers)**: Collection of sayings on ethical and moral conduct.

10. **Horayot (Decisions)**: Deals with cases in which the Bet Din or High Priest erred or a King of Israel committed an error.

Fifth Order: Kodshim (Holy Things): This order is devoted to laws pertaining to the sacrifices and to the Temple. Following are the tractates in this fifth order:

1. **Zevachim (Animal Sacrifices)**: Deals with various animal sacrifices.

2. **Menahot (Meal Offerings)**: Deals with various meal offerings as well as the laws of tallit,(prayer shawl) tefillin (phylacteries) and mezuzah.

3. **Hullin (Ordinary)**: Deals with non sacrificial regulations, namely the slaughter of animals for ordinary consumption.

4. **Bekhorot (Firstlings)**: Deals with laws concerning firstborn male animals and their possible blemishes.

5. **Arakhin (Valuations)**: Deals with laws regarding dedicatory vows of valuation and other laws of dedicating objects to the Temple.

6. **Temurah (Substitution)**: Deals with laws governing the substitution of one sacrifice for another.

7. **Keritot (Excisions)**: Deals with sins,

which if committed intentionally, incur the punishment of excision.

8. **Me'ilah (Sacrilege)**: Deals with laws concerning the unlawful use of objects that have been consecrated to the Temple.

9. **Tamid (Daily Sacrifice)**: Deals with permanent laws of Temple and procedures regarding the regular daily sacrifice.

10. **Middot (Measurements)**: Deals with the plan of the Second Temple and the measurement of its sections.

11. **Kinnin (Birds' nests)**: Deals with sacrifices of birds offered as a sin offering or burnt offering.

Sixth Order: Teharot (Purity): Deals with laws of ritual purity and impurity. The following are the tractates in this sixth order:

1. **Kelim (Vessels)**; Deals with various forms of ritual impurity that applies to utensils.

2. **Ohalot (Tents)**: Deals with the ritual impurity of a tent containing a dead body.

3. **Nega'im (Leprosy)**: Deals with laws of leprosy.

4. **Parah (Heifer)**: Deals with laws regarding the red heifer.

5. **Teharot (Purifications)**: Deals with laws of ritual impurity.

6. **Mikvaot (Ritual baths)**: Deals with laws of ritual baths.

7. **Niddah (Menstruating woman)**: Deals with ritual impurity of a menstruating woman.

8. **Machshirin: (Predispositions)**: Deals with how foods become susceptible to ritual impurity by contact with certain liquids.

9. **Zavim (Those suffering from secretions):** Deals with laws of ritual impurity of those suffering from gonorrhea, secretions and seminal emissions.

10. **Tevul Yom (Immersed during the Day)**: Deals with laws governing ritual impurity of someone who has immersed himself in a ritual bath during the day, but who does not attain ritual purity in the evening.

11. **Yadayim (Hands)**: Deals with laws concerning washing of hands.

12. **Uktzin (Stems)**: Deals with laws governing ritual impurity of stems and the fruits attached to them.

MINOR TRACTATES OF THE TALMUD

The following are a listing and brief summary of the Minor Tractates of the Talmud:

1. **Avot of Rabbi Natan:** A supplement to the Ethics of the fathers, consisting of more ethical sayings.
2. **Soferim (Scribes)**: Laws governing Torah scrolls and how they must be written.
3. **Semahot (Happy Occasions)**: Euphemistic name of tractate dealing with laws of mourning.
4. **Kallah (Bride)**: Deals with laws of marriage and sexual relations.
5. **Kallah Rabbati (Long Tractate on Brides)**: Deals with laws of personal behavior and what manners befit a Jew, especially a scholar.
6. **Derech Eretz Rabbah**: **(Longer Tractate on Courtesy)**: Deals with laws of courtesy and with general ethics.

7. **Derech Eretz Zuta (Short Tractate on Courtesy)**: Deals with manners and behavior appropriate to a scholar.

8. **Gerim (Converts)**: Deals with laws governing converts.

9. **Kutim (Samaritans)**: Deals with laws applying to the Samaritans, a sect viewed as between a Jew and a non-Jew.

10. **Avadim (Slaves)**: Deals with laws governing Hebrew slaves.

11. **Sefer Torah (Torah Scroll)**: Deals with laws of writing a Torah scroll.

12. **Tefillin (Phylacteries)**: Deals with laws of head and arm phylacteries.

12. **Tzitzit (Fringes)**: Deals with laws of ritual fringes.

13. **Mezuzah**: Deals with laws of writing the parchment scroll placed on doorposts and the manner in which it must be affixed.

CODES OF JEWISH LAW

The sea of Talmud was so vast that it was often difficult for a person to locate all specific references on any given subject. This situation led the rabbis to begin to codify the laws and set them in order, according to subject matter, so that one would be able to find them more easily. Following are several important law codes:

1. Mishneh Torah: Assembled by Moses Maimonides in the twelfth century, this fourteen volume law code arranged in a methodical and logical manner the laws of the Talmud.

2. Arba'ah Turim ("The Four Rows") Arranged by Rabbi Jacob ben Asher using the method of Maimonides, he arranged the laws by classification rather than location. His work consisted of these four parts: i. Orach Chayim, dealing with laws of prayer and a person's daily conduct.

ii. Yoreh Deah, dealing with the dietary laws, laws of ritual purity and mourning.

iii. Even Haezer, dealing with personal and family matters, including laws of marriage and divorce.

iv. Choshen Mishpat, dealing with criminal and civil law.

3. Shulchan Aruch ("The Prepared Table"): By far the most popular, respected and authoritative laws code was that edited by Rabbi Joseph Karo in the sixteenth century. This work is actually an abbreviated and simplified form of the Arba'ah Turim, taking into account the views of previous codifiers. This code deals with Jewish law and practice wherever the Jew might be—at home, in the synagogue or at business.

With the publication of the Shulchan Aruch, the period of scholars known as the "Rishonim" (first ones) ended and the period of the "Acharonim" (later ones) began. From the end of the 16th century to the present the acharonim have issued authoritative interpretations of the law.

MIDRASH

Midrash is the process by which Jews in every generation have grappled with the underlying significance of biblical texts. It contains homiletical interpretation of the Bible, sermonic teachings, ethical maxims, popular sayings and legends. The best known is the "Midrash Rabbah" ("Great Midrash"), consisting of ten books of homiletic interpretation of the Five Books of Moses and the Five Megillot. Another is the "Midrash Tanchuma", named after Rabbi Tanchuma bar Abba in the fourth century.

RESPONSA

Responsa are written replies given to questions about all aspects of Jewish law by qualified authorities from the Talmudic period to the present. The questions asked by the individuals of their rabbis were often based on some current situation which was not directly dealt with in the earlier codes. For instance, is it permissible to use a life-sustaining device to keep a patient alive? The rabbi would given his responsum (answer) based on his reasoning on support statements and earlier precedents found in the Bible, Talmud and Shulchan Aruch. In this way Jewish law continued to develop, change and be modified in order to be in consonance with new times and new situations.

JEWISH SOCIAL, RELIGIOUS AND POLITICAL MOVEMENTS IN A NUTSHELL

This chapter briefly presents the major Jewish social, religious and political movements from early times to the present.

The Five Books of Moses begins the story of the Jews. It is traditionally understood as the inspired book given by God to the Israelites through Moses, the father of the prophets, first in the desert, and then again in the plains of Moab. Principally, it teaches the commandments and laws by which the Jews, God's chosen people, are to live in the Promised Land which God had promised to the patriarchs Abraham, Isaac and Jacob. The Five Books of Moses also presents a brief account of Jewish history from its earliest beginnings. The includes the story of God's revelation to the patriarchs and His covenant with them, the descent to Egypt, the exodus, the events in the forty years in the wilderness.

In the Desert (1300 B.C.E): Political life in the desert was expressed by two groups. One group of Israelites advocated a life of independence by conquering the land of Canaan. The other group, a source of trouble to Moses, advocated a return to Egypt. This latter group was eliminated during the forty years of wandering in the desert.

In the Time of Judges: After the death of Joshua, successor to Moses, there were two political trends. One opposed unity of the tribes. It was dominated by the heads of the tribes of Judah and Ephraim, who were rivals for national leadership. The minority advocated a united nation under one ruler. For about two hundred years, until the days of Samuel, the tribes were independent of each other.

In the Time of Samuel: During Samuel's rule as judge, he succeeded in uniting the twelve tribes of Israel. When Samuel grew old, there was a demand for a King. With God's advice, Samuel chose Saul as Israel's first king.

In the Time of Saul: Saul's reign found factions fighting for control of the land. There was the House of Saul and the House of David. After Saul and his three sons were killed in battle with the Philistines, David became King over Judah. The remainder of Israel was under the nominal rule of Ish Boshet, son of Saul. Several years later David was made king over all Israel.

Secession Movement: The secessionists, under the leadership of Jeroboam, revolted against Solomon (from the tribe of Judah) but were put to flight. Jeroboam fled to Egypt . When Solomon died and his son Rehoboam became king, Jeroboam managed to get ten tribes to form a separate kingdom under the name of Israel. He then became their first king. Now the kingdom which David and Solomon had built was divided.

The First Temple: During the first Temple, political opinion was divided among pro-Aramean, pro-Assyrian and pro-Egyptian groups. In Israel the prophets warned against foreign mergers. The rulers ignored their advice and entered an alliance with Egypt against Babylon. The result was the conquest of Judea by Babylon.

In the Days of Ezra and Nehemiah: After Babylon was defeated by the Persians and King Cyrus, the Jews were allowed to return to Judea. The majority of Jews who lived in Babylon remained there, becoming quite prosperous. A small minority under the leadership of Ezra and Nehemiah returned, building a new life in Judea.

In the Days of the Maccabees: There were two parties in Judea at this time—the Hellenists, under the leadership of Jason, adopted Greek customs. And the Hasidim, the pietists, under the leadership of Mattathias and his five sons, who advocated preservation of Jewish customs. Although the Maccabees were in the minority, they defeated the Syrian-Greeks and won religious freedom. The holiday of Hanukkah each year commemorates the victory of the Maccabees and the purification of the Temple.

Hyrkan and Aristobulus: After the death of Queen Shlomit of Alexandria of the Hasmonean house (established by the Maccabees), her two sons fought for power. Hyrkan favored the Romans. Aristobulus favored an independent policy, not trusting Rome. Hyrkan invited the Romans to help him against his own brother. Pompey, the Roman consul, took advantage of this to put an end to Judean independence.

Religious and Political Parties before the Destruction of Second Temple: There were three religious parties in Judea as well as two political parties:

1. Pharisees (from the word "parush" meaning to separate) They consisted of the bulk of the laity and the poor. They advocated the country to be governed by the Torah laws, and rabbinic law to be respected. They advocated belief in life after death, popular education and development of the liturgy.

2. Sadducees (after originator, Zadok). They consisted of the wealthy class and advocated civil law above religious law, strict interpretation of the Torah and disregard for belief in an afterlife.

3. Essenes: They were fishermen and farmers, advocating an ascetic life, strict observance of the law, and joint ownership of property.

4. Zealots: They consisted of many young Jews who were against Roman rule. They advocated a fight to the finish and lost to the Romans.

5. The Boethusians: Composed of the wealthy pro-Roman politicians, they advocated complete submission to Rome.

Rabbinical and Karaite Movements: During the period of the Gaonim, the Jews were split by two factions, the Rabbinites and the Karaites. The Rabbinites advocated observance of Torah laws and also laws passed by sages of the Talmud. The Karaites, organized by Anan ben David advocated strict observance of the Torah laws without the need for rabbinic interpretation. The Rabbinites won and excluded the Karaites from the Jewish community.

Kabbalah Mystical Movement: This movement advocated soul purification through good deeds and concentrated study of Torah. Its originators included Rabbi Joseph Karo (author of the Shulchan Aruch), Rabbi Cordovero and Rabbi Isaac Luria, known as the Ari. Rabbi Vital, student of Luria, spread the mystical ideal of the kabbalah throughout Europe using the

Book of the Zohar (said to have been written by Rabbi Simon bar Yochai of the second century)

Shabataen: Shabbati Zevi, a self appointed Messiah (17th century) was leader of this movement. It was the largest and most significant messianic movement in Jewish history since the failed Bar Kokhba rebellion. It climaxed in 1666 when Zevi converted to Islam.

Frankism: Organized by Jacob Frank, who claimed to be the reincarnation of Shabbatai Zevi. Frank and his followers ended by becoming Catholics.

Hasidism: This movement is based on the belief that simple worship is most acceptable to God. It was advocated that prayers ought to be service of the heart and that people should approach God with joy, happiness and song. The Hasidim looked upon their rabbis for advice and help. In essence, they were intermediaries between themselves and God. Its chief exponent was Rabbi Israel Baal Shem Tov (called the Besht). His follower, Rabbi Shneur Zalman, made Hasidism a part of Jewish life throughout the world.

Mitnagdim: Those opposing the Hasidim were the Mitnagdim, who head was Rabbi Elijah Gaon of Vilna. He claimed that only an educated person can, by knowing and understanding the laws, be a pious Jew. He also claimed that worshiping Hasidic rabbis is against the Jewish idea of equality among all people

Haskalah: The Haskalah or enlightenment movement flourished in the 18th and 19th centuries. The Maskilim (Enlighteners) advocated secular education among Jews rather than religious studies. They favored use of Hebrew language not only for prayer but for use in daily living.

Musar Movement: This movement advocates the supremacy of ethics of the Torah

and the Talmud. It was founded by Rabbi
Israel Lipkin, called the Salanter, after the
town of Salant where he was rabbi. Based
on both Torah and the Talmud, these ethics
stipulated that one should think good and
practice goodness

Chafetz Chayim: Rabbi Israel Meyer
Hakohen, known as the Chafetz Chayim,
advocated the idea that one should refrain
from criticizing others and should first crit-
icize oneself. His most famous work was a
book on "lashon hara"—evil talk. It was
called "Shemirat HaLashon." He also
wrote a six volume work called the "Mishna
Berurah", consisting of laws of daily Jewish
practice.

HIGHLIGHTS OF ISRAELI
HISTORY—A TIMELINE

Middle Bronze Age (Patriarchs)	2200–1500 B.C.E.
Late Bronze Age (Moses and Joshua)	1550–1200 B.C.E.
Iron Age (Israelite)	1200–587 B.C.E.
Destruction of First Temple	587 B.C.E.
Babylonian and Persian Period	587–322 B.C.E.
Hellenic Period	322–167 B.C.E.
Hasmonean Period	167–63 B.C.E.
Roman Period	63B.C.E–324C.E.
Destruction of Second Temple	70 C.E.
Byzantine Period (Christianity)	324–640 C.E.
Persian Conquest	614–628 C.E.
Arab-Moslem Period	640–1099 C.E.
Crusader Period	1099–1291 C.E.
Mameluke Period (Moslems)	1291–1516 C.E.

First Jewish Colony	1878 C.E.
First Zionist Congress	1897 C.E.
British Mandate	1917–1948 C.E.
State of Israel	May 14, 1948
Sinai Campaign	1957
Six Day War	1967
Yom Kippur War	1973

HOW ISRAEL ACHIEVED STATEHOOD (1838–1948) IN A NUTSHELL

1838	Moses Montefiore proposes founding a Jewish state
1854	Jewish hospital established in Jerusalem
1861	Mishkenot Sha'ananim, the first neighborhood outside Jerusalem City walls is built
1863	First Hebrew periodical, "Havazelet" published
1878	Petach Tikveh established
1882	Large scale immigration from Russia and Yemen begins (known as First Aliyah)
1897	World Zionist Organization Founded
1904	Second wave of immigration to Israel begins from Poland and Russia
1909	Deganya, Israel's first kibbutz established

1917	Balfour Declaration pledges British support for Jewish national home in Palestine
1919	Third wave of immigration begins, mainly from Poland
1924	Technion, Israel's Institute of Science opens in Haifa. Fourth wave of immigration to Israel.
1925	Hebrew University established
1933	Fifth wave of immigration, from Germany
1940	Jews from Palestine fight with British army against Nazis
1945	World War II ends
1947	United Nations partition plan for Palestine is accepted by Jews but rejected by Arabs
1948	End of British Mandate. State of Israel is officially proclaimed.

AMERICAN JEWRY HIGHLIGHTS

1620: First Jewish Colony in the New World. The Jews settled in Brazil during the period when it was captured by the Dutch. They formed the first colony in Recife. In 1680 Samuel Nasi bought an island and founded a Jewish colony which he called Jewish Savannah.

1654: First Jews in New Amsterdam: In 1654, 23 Jews arrived in New Amsterdam, fleeing from Portuguese inquisition in Brazil. The Jews established their first cemetery in 1655, in New Amsterdam, near what is now Chatham Square. They organized their first central congregation in New York in 1685. Their first synagogue was the Shearith Israel on Mill Street, built in 1730. Today it exists as the Spanish Portuguese Synagogue on Central Park West in New York City.

1655: First Demand for Equal Rights in New Amsterdam. Asher Levy demanded equal rights with the other burghers to serve in the guard. Peter Stuyvesant, governor of New Amsterdam, refused to grant the request. The question was brought before the stockholders of the West Indies Company in Holland, several of whom were Jews. Thereafter the Jews of New Amsterdam were recognized as full citizens.

Early Jewish Settlements in the U.S.
1656: First Jew, Jacob Lumbrozo, settled in Baltimore
1726: Jews settled in Pennsylvania
1733: Portuguese Jews arrive in Georgia

Jews Active in the War for Independence: There were nine Jews among the merchants who signed the Non-Importation agreement of Philadelphia on Oct. 25, 1765. The signers agreed not to import goods from England until Great Britain abandoned the impositions on the Colonies.

Francis Salvador: In 1776, he was the first Jew to die in the American Revolution. He was also the first Jew to hold state office in America, elected as member of first Provincial Congress of South Carolina in 1774.

Colonel David S. Franks and Mordecai Sheftel: These men played important military roles in the Revolutionary War.

Gershom Mendes Seixas: The Rabbi of the Shearith Israel Synagogue, he followed his congregation to Philadelphia where he worked tirelessly for the revolutionary cause.

Hayim Solomon: This Polish Jew raised funds for Washington's army and gave financial aid to members of the Continental Congress, including James Madison.

Benjamin Nones: He served under General Washington, and was one of a number of Jews who supported Thomas Jefferson and the Democratic-Republican movement which he led.

Jews in the Civil War: The majority of Jews sided with the North on the slavery issue. There was a minority which sided with the Confederates. Among those strongly supporting Lincoln were Lewis Dembitz, Abraham Kohn and Abraham Jones

Waves of Immigration: The first arrival was the landing of Jews in New Amsterdam. They came from Brazil and were mostly Spanish-Portuguese Jews.
Between 1848 and 1890, German and Western European Jews emigrated to the U.S. to escape oppression.
In 1890, large numbers of Eastern European Jews began to arrive from Lithuania, Poland and Russia.
Waves of Jewish Immigration to the U.S.

1880–1890	193,000
1890–1900	393,000
1901–1910	976,000

In 1932, with the coming of Adolf Hitler, a fourth wave of German Jews began. After World War II in 1945, a fifth wave began of displaced Eastern European Jews

JEWISH ORGANIZATIONAL LIFE IN AMERICA

Jewish social and organized life in America took different turns with each new wave of immigration. When the Sephardic (Spanish) Jews arrived, they organized their social circles around their synagogue, cemetery and educational activities. The German Jews organized their social and religious life on a more elaborate scale. They organized a seminary of Rabbis, fraternal organizations and the Hebrew Immigrant Aid society, which takes care of new immigrants.

Following is a partial list of Jewish Religious, Social and Political Organizations in America:

1.   **American Jewish Committee (AJC)**: Organization to prevent the infraction of the civil and religious rights of the Jews throughout the world.

2. **American Jewish Congress**: Aim is to preserve and promote the democratic way of life and to encourage Jewish education.

3. **AntiDefamation League**: Purpose is to fight antisemitism and anti Jewish discrimination.

4. **B'nai Brith**: National fraternal order whose purpose was to provide mutual aid and insurance. Today it is also involved in philanthropy and political action for the protection of Jewish rights.

5. **Bureaus of Jewish Education**: Serves individual communities as Boards of Jewish Education.

6. **Council of Jewish Federations (CJF)**: The national body coordinating the work of all of its members Jewish Federations.

7. **Free Loan Society**: Philanthropic

organization that helps needy by offering interest free loans.

8. **Hadassah**: Women's organization and largest Zionist organization in the U.S., it promotes Jewish institutions and health related enterprises in Israel.

9. **Hebrew Union College—Jewish Institute of Religion**: School to train rabbis, cantors and educators of the Reform movement.

10. **Hillel Foundations**: Program of service on college campuses.

11. **Jewish Community Center**: Recreational, cultural and social centers.

12. **Jewish Federation**: Raises and distributes funds for local, national and overseas needs.

13. **Jewish Theological Seminary**:

School that trains rabbis, cantors and educators for the Conservative Movement.

14. **Joint Distribution Committee**: Raises money and dispenses it for the relief of war victims. Also finds homes for refugees and provides medical care for orphan children.

15. **National Community Relations Advisory Council (NCRAC)**: National community defense agency that monitors anti-Jewish feelings and acts.

16. **National Council of Jewish Women**: Undertakes a wide range of activities for the better of the Jewish community and the community at large.

17. **Reconstructionist Rabbinical College**: Rabbinical school for the Reconstructionist movement.

18. **Synagogue Council of America:**

Body that represents major Jewish movements in America.

19. **United Jewish Appeal (UJA)**: Provides financial support for Jews overseas and resettlement in Israel and elsewhere.

20. **Yeshiva University**: Institution of higher learning that trains teachers and rabbis for the Orthodox branch of Judaism.

21. **Young Men's Young Women's Hebrew Association (YM/YWHA)**: Provides recreational and cultural opportunities.

21. **Zionist Organization of America (ZOA)**: Organization of Zionist that helps with fundraising and public relations for the State of Israel.

MAJOR RELIGIOUS
MOVEMENTS IN AMERICA

Orthodox Judaism: A synonym for traditional Judaism, which acknowledges divine revelation of Torah and the binding authority of Jewish law.

Conservative Judaism: The organized institutionalized system of Judaism that follows the Historical School. It maintains a traditional view on law, which holds that contemporary decisions should be fixed by a body of rabbinical experts and interpreted by local rabbis. Conservative Judaism holds that the religious legal tradition must be held in reverence, but that the need for changes and modifications must be recognized and addressed when they become pressing.

Reform Judaism: The first modern movement to develop as a result of the changes in

Europe brought about as a result of emancipation. While there is a variance of agreement of Reform Jews regarding individual customs and practices, there is agreement concerning the legitimacy of change and the fact that no formulation has eternal validity.

Reconstructionist Judaism: The institutionalized movement whose foundation and infrastructure emanate from the philosophy of Mordecai Kaplan, its founder. Kaplan argued that Jewish beliefs have broken down, and Jewish identity, therefore, needs to be nurtured so that the Jewish historical belief in salvation in the world to come, which has kept him alive, can be transformed into salvation in this world. Kaplan further defined Judaism as an evolving civilization whose common denominator is the continuous life of the Jewish people.

TIME LINE OF JEWISH PERSONALITIES AND EVENTS

Date	Event	Important People
B.C.E.		
1900	Abraham worships one God	Abraham, Isaac, Sarah and Rebekah
1750	Abraham's great grandchildren leave Israel and go to Egypt	Jacob, Rachel, Leah and Joseph
1450	Ten Plagues: Pharaoh releases Israelite slaves	Moses, Miriam, Aaron
1410–1050	Israel conquers Canaan, settles down in tribes ruled by Judges	Joshua, Deborah, Samuel
1050–933	Saul unifies tribes; David enlarges kingdom. Solomon builds First Temple	Samuel, David, Saul, Solomon and Nathan

Date	Event	Important People
928	Kingdom splits in two: Israel in north. Judea in south. Prophets try to teach people to listen to God's word	Elijah, Amos, Micah
722	Assyria conquers northern kingdom, and takes it people captives	Isaiah
586	Babylonians conquer Judea and destroy Temple. Babylonian exile begins	Jeremiah,Ezekiel
538	Cyrus permits return to Judea. Temple rebuilt	Esther, Ezra, Nehemiah
322	Judea becomes immersed in Greek culture (Hellenism)	

Date	Event	Important People
168–164	Antiochus driven out by Maccabees; Temple cleansed	Hannah, Mattathias, Judah Maccabee
63	Romans conquer Judea	Herod

C.E.

30	Romans kill Jesus. His followers begin to spread Christianity throughout empire.	Philo Hillel/Shammai
66–73	Jewish revolt against Rome; last Jewish rebels die at Masada.	Simeon bar Giora, Johanan ben Zakkai
132–135	Second Jewish revolt against Rome. Jews continue to pray and study in secret.	Akiba ben Joseph, Bar Kokhba Meir, Beruriah, Simeon bar Yohai

Date	Event	Important People
210	Center of Jewish study shifts to Babylon. Mishneh edited by Judah the Prince	Judah HaNasi, Samuel
400–500	Babylonian Jews build academies. Gemara is completed.	Rav Ashi, Rabina
622	Muhammad founds Islam in Arabia	
740–970	Judaism spreads as far as Russia, where Khazar kingdom coverts	Saadia Gaon Hasdai ibn Shaprut
950–1391	Spain is new center of Jewish life	Samuel HaNagid, Solomon ibn Gabirol, Judah HaLevi
950–1100	Jews settle in England, France and Germany	Rashi Gershom ben Judah and Maimonides

Date	Event	Important People
	where Gershom and Rashi study and comment on Jewish law	
1096–1320	Crusaders drive Muslims out of Palestine and destroy many Jewish communities	Meir of Rothenberg
1200–1400	Jews persecuted in Western Europe	
1348–1349	Black Plague. Increasing oppression in Spain	Moses de Leon, Joseph Albo
1492	Expulsion of Jews from Spain.	
1500–1600	Spanish and Portuguese Jews flee to Italy, North Africa and New World. Find welcome in Turkish Empire and Palestine.	Joseph Karo, Joseph Nasi, Gracia Mendes

Date	Event	Important People
	Code of Jewish Law completed by Joseph Karo	
1400–1648	Jews live peacefully in Poland, governed by Council of Four Lands	Moses Isserles, Solomon Luria
1648–1658	Cossacks in Poland revolt and destroy hundreds of Jewish communities	
1665–1676	False Messiah Shabbati Zevi brings hope to desperate Polish Jews	Shabbati Zevi
1500–1700	Marranos move north to Holland and France to practice Judaism freely. Jews begin to return to England.	Manasseh ben Israel
1654	Twenty three Jews come to New Amsterdam from Brazil	Asser Levy Jacob Barsimson

Date	Event	Important People
1750's	Hasidism emerges as a religious revolt	Israel Baal Shem Tov Shneur Zalman of Liady; Vilna Gaon
1787	U.S. Constitution promises religious freedom to all. France gives equal rights to Jews	Haym Solomon, Aaron Lopez, Rebecca Gratz
1800–1900	Equal rights spread in Western Europe; pogroms in E. Europe	Moses Montefiore, Mayer Rothschild, Judah Leib Gordon, Sholem Aleichem
1981	Pogroms in Russia; Jews begin emigrating to Western Europe and America. Modern Zionists go to Palestine	Moses Hess, First Edmond de Rothschild
1894	Dreyfus falsely accused of treason in France	

Date	Event	Important People
1897	First Zionist Congress	Leo Pinsker, Theodor Herzl
1900–1914	Pogroms drive more Russian Jews to Western Europe, America and Palestine	Emma Lazarus, Lillian Wald
1917	Britain issues Balfour Declaration. More Jews settle in Palestine.	Ahad HaAm, Louis Brandeis
1933	Nazis gain power in Germany. Jews persecuted	Leo Baeck, Stephen Wise, Henriettta Szold
1939–1945	World War II. By 1945, six million Jews are killed.	Mordecai Anielewicz, Janusz Korczak
1948	State of Israel established.	David Ben Gurion, Chaim Weizmann
1967	Israel wins Six Day War, Jerusalem reunified.	Moshe Dayan, Yigal Allon

Date	Event	Important People
1973	Yom Kippur War	Golda Meir, Arik Sharon
1979	Egypt and Israel sign Camp David Accords	Menahem Begin
1980's	Mass Exodus of Ethiopian and Soviet Jews	

JEWISH LIFE CYCLE

The major life cycle events of a Jew are birth, circumcision for a boy, Hebrew naming for both boys and girls, Pidyon HaBen (Redemption of First Born), Bar and Bat Mitzvah, Confirmation, Marriage and Death. Following are the terms related to each of these life cycle events.

Glossary of Terms

Judaism has its own vocabulary, including terms for customs and ceremonies, holidays, rituals and life cycle events. Many terms and phrases and in Hebrew or Yiddish. Here is a list of frequently used words and phrases.

Aliyah: The honor of being called to recite the Torah blessings during the synagogue Torah reading.

Aron HaKodesh: Holy Ark, the place in which the Torah scrolls are kept.

Beit Knesset.: House of assembly, today it means the synagogue.

Bimah: Platform-pulpit area in a synagogue.

Haftarah: Conclusion. The prophetic section recited after the reading of the Torah on Sabbaths, Festivals and other occasions.

Hazzan: Cantor

Kippah: Skullcap.

Mahzor: Prayerbook used on Rosh Hashanah and Yom kippur. Also special prayerbook for one of the three Pilgrimage Festivals.

Minyan: Quorum of ten adults needed for public prayer service.

Ner Tamid Eternal Light. Light above ark which is always kept burning.

Oneg Shabbat: Shabbat Enjoyment. Celebration after Friday evening services which often includes refreshments, singing and Israeli dancing.

Rav: Rabbi

Sefer Torah: The Torah scroll, consisting of the Five Books of Moses: Genesis, Exodus, Leviticus, Numbers and Deuteronomy.

Shamash: Sexton or Ritual Director

Shul: Synagogue (Yiddish)

Siddur: (Prayerbook)

Sidra: The weekly portion of the Torah that is read aloud at services.

Tallit: Prayer shawl worn during morning prayer services and on Kol Nidrei eve, the night of the Day of Atonement.

Holiday Terms

The Shabbat: (The Sabbath)

Besamim: Spices during the Havdalah service.

Hallah: See Food Terms

Erev Shabbat: The eve of the Sabbath (Friday evening)

Hamotzi: Blessing said over bread.

Havdalah: Separation. Service on Saturday

night that bids farewell to the Sabbath.

Kabbalat Shabbat: Welcoming the Sabbath. Service just before the evening service on Friday night.

Kiddush: Sanctification. The blessing over the wine, recited on Friday evening and Saturday morning.

Motza-ey Shabbat. The departure of the Sabbath.

Seudah Shelisheet: The Third meal, eaten during late Sabbath afternoon between the Mincha afternoon service and Ma'ariv evening service.

Shabbat Shalom: Sabbath Peace. A Sabbath greeting.

Shaharit: The morning service.

Shomer Shabbat: A Sabbath observer.

Zemirot: Sabbath or festival songs sung at the table.

Rosh Hashanah and Yom Kippur

Al Heit: Opening words, and hence the title, of Yom Kippur confessional prayer.

Aseret Y'may Teshuvah: Ten Days of Repentance, from Rosh Hashanah to Yom Kippur. Also known as the Days of Awe.

Baal Toke'ah: Person who sounds the shofar.

Gemar hatimah tovah: "May your final verdict be a favorable one." Greeting for the days after Rosh Hashanah.

High Holy Days: Rosh Hashanah and Yom Kippur, and the days in between.

Kol Nidrei: Liturgical text which ushers in Yom Kippur.

Leshanah tova tikateivu: "May you be inscribed for a good year." A greeting for Rosh Hashanah.

Mahzor: Festival prayerbook.

Neila: Closing service of Yom Kippur

Selihot: Prayers of forgiveness recited during High Holy Days. Also refers to penitential service beginning at midnight on Saturday preceding Rosh Hashanah.

Shofar: Ram's horn.

Shevarim: Three blasts of the shofar.

Tekiah: One blast of the shofar.

Tekiah Gedolah: One very long shofar blast.

Teruah: Nine short blasts of the shofar.

Teshuvah: Repentance.

Yamim Noraim: The Days of Awe.

Sukkot, Shemini Atzeret, Simhat Torah

Aravot: Long narrow willow leaves attached to lulav on the left side.

Etrog: Citron, one of four species used during Sukkot.

Four Species: Arba Minim in Hebrew. Collective term for etrog, lulav, (palm) aravot (willow) and hadassim (myrtle) used on Sukkot.

Hadassim: Myrtle leaves attached to lulav on the right side.

Hag Sameiah: Happy holiday, a festival greeting.

Hakafot: Processions around sanctuary with Torah scroll on Simhat Torah.

Hatan Beresheet: "Bridegroom of Genesis". Special honor on Simhat Torah of being called up for first sidrah in annual cycle of Torah readings.

Hatan Torah: "Bridegroom of Torah." Special honor on Simhat Torah of being called up for last sidra in annual cycle of Torah readings.

Hol Hamoed: Intermediate days of a festival.

Kol Ha'ne'arim: Refers to the calling up of all children on Simchat Torah to stand under the tallit for the group aliyah.

Lulav: Palm branch, one of the four species.

S'khakh: Greens covering the roof of the sukkah.

Sukkah: Booth used on Sukkot.

Yizkor: Memorial Prayer for the dead recited on or near last day of every major festival.

Hanukkah

Al HaNissim: Special prayer of deliverance.

Antiochus: Syrian king who forbade Jews to practice their religion.

Dreidel. ("Sevivon" in Hebrew): Four-sided top used in Hanukkah games.

Hallel: Psalms of praise to God recited on Hanukkah, Rosh Hodesh and Pilgrimage Festivals.

Hanukkah: Festival of Dedication, lasting for eight days.

Hanukkah gelt: Money given to children as a Hanukkah gift.

Hanukkiah: Hanukkah candelabrum, also called a Hanukkah menorah.

Kislev: Hebrew month in which Hanukkah falls.

Latkes: See food terms.

Maoz Tzur: "Rock of Ages". Popular hymn sung on Hanukkah.

Nun, Gimel, Hay and Shin: Hebrew letters on the dreidel. They stand for the Hebrew words "nes gadol haya sham", meaning "a great miracle happened there."

Shamash: Special "servant" candle used to light the other candles in the hanukkiah.

Tevet: Hebrew month in which Hanukkah ends.

Purim

Adar: Hebrew month during which Purim occurs.

Ahasuerus: King of Persia involved in Purim story.

Esther: Wife of Ahasuerus and heroine of Purim story. The Scroll of Esther is read during the Purim service.

Gragger (ra'ashan in Hebrew): Noisemaker used during the Megillah reading to drown out Haman's name.

Hadassah: Esther's Hebrew name.

Haman: Prime minister of Ahasuerus. He tried to persuade the king to permit pogroms against Persian Jews. Instead, he was hung.

Hamantaschen: See food terms.

Mattanot l'evyonim: Gifts to the poor on Purim.

Mordecai: Cousin of Esther and hero of Purim story.

Pur: Lot cast to determine one's fate. Name of holiday comes from its plural form "purim."

Seudah: Special feast associated with a holiday or Jewish life cycle event.

Shushan: City where story of Purim took place.

Shushan Purim: The day after Purim (the fifteenth of Adar), ordained by the Jews in Persia's capital and in walled cities.

Ta'anit Esther: Fast of Esther, observed the day before Purim from dawn to dusk, in commemoration of the fast that Esther imposed upon herself.

Vashti: Rebellious queen of King Ahasuerus.

Passover

Afikoman: Piece of matzah hidden at beginning of Seder, to be found by the children.

Bedikat Hametz: Search for unleavened bread on night before Passover.

Beitzah: See Food Terms.

Biur Hametz: Burning of hametz on morning before Passover.

Four Questions: Questions asked by youngest child during early part of Seder.

Had Gadya: "One kid." A favorite seder song.

Haggadah: Book used at Passover seder.

Hametz: See Food Terms

Haroset: See Food Terms

Karpas: See Food Terms

Mah Nishtanah: Opening words of Four Questions

Ma-ot Hittim: Special matzah fund used to help needy before Passover.

Maror: See Food Terms

Matzah: See Food Terms

Moadim Lesimhah: "Joyous Festival." A Festival greeting.

Nisan: Month when exodus from Egypt took place.

Seder: Festive meal and ceremony held on first two nights of Passover (first night only in Israel and for Reform Jews)

Zeroa: See Food Terms

Shavuot

Akdamut: Special liturgical poem read during Shavuot services.

Bikkurim: First fruits brought to Temple as Shavuot offering.

Blintz: See Food Terms.

Feast of Weeks: Another name for Shavuot.

Sivan: Hebrew month in which Shavuot occurs.

Tikkun Leil Shavuot: Study session on night of Shavuot.

Jewish Food Terms

Beitzah: Roasted egg on Seder plate, a symbol of life.

Blintz: Thin crepe-like pancake filled with cottage cheese, potatoes or fruit. Often served on Shavuot.

Borsht: Beet soup often served with sour cream or boiled potato.

Hallah: Braided bread used on Sabbaths and Festivals.

Fleishig (Yiddish): Foods prepared with meat or meat products; in accordance with the dietary laws, they may not be eaten with dairy (milchig) foods.

Gefilte Fish: Stuffed fish, often served as first course of Sabbath or holiday meal.

Hametz: Foods containing leavened grains, forbidden on Passover.

Haroset: Mixture of apples, cinnamon, nuts and wine served on Passover, symbolizing mortar used to make bricks in Egypt.

Hamantachen: Triangular pockets of dough filled with poppy seeds or jam served on Purim.

Karpas: Greens (usually parsley) on Seder plate, symbolizing spring. Some people use potatoes for karpas.

Kneidel: Matzah-meal dumpling, often added to chicken broth. Sometimes called matzah ball.

Kosher: Refers to foods that are fit to be eaten according to Jewish dietary laws.

Kreplach: Triangular dumplings often filled with meat and served with soup.

Kugel: Noodle or potato pudding.

Latke: (**levivah**, in Hebrew): Potato pancake, traditionally eaten on Hanukkah.

Maror: Bitter herbs, usually horseradish, served as Passover Seder.

Matzah: Unleavened bread eaten during Passover.

Milchig (Yiddish): Foods prepared with milk or other dairy products; in accordance with dietary laws, they may not be eaten with, or immediately after, meat (fleishig) foods.

Pareve (Yiddish): Foods that are neither fleishig nor milchig, but neutral according to dietary laws; e.g. fruits and vegetables.

Zeroa: Roasted lamb shankbone symbolizing Passover sacrifice in ancient Temple.

Life Cycle Terms

Birth and Education

Bar Mitzvah (masc), Bat Mitzvah (fem): One who is responsible for observing the mitzvot (religious commandments). For boys, this occurs at age thirteen, for girls at age twelve.

Brit Milah: Circumcision ceremony occurring on eighth day after birth of Jewish boy.

Confirmation: Ceremony often tied to Shavuot in which teenagers confirm their acceptance to Judaism.

Kohen: Descendant of ancient priestly tribe. Conducts Pidyon HaBen ceremony for firstborn and receives honor of first aliyah at services.

Kvater (masc) and Kvaterin (fem): Godfather and godmother, appointed at time of circumcision.

Mohel (masc), Mohelet (fem): Person who performs surgery during ritual circumcision.

Pidyon HaBen: Ceremony for redemption of first born.

Sandek: Person who holds child at ritual circumcision.

Simhat Bat: Naming ceremony of newborn Jewish girl.

Shalom Zakhar/Shalom Nekeivah: Ceremony welcoming newborn Jewish child (boy or girl), often held on first Friday evening after the birth.

Marriage

Aufruf: Calling of the groom-to-be (and often bride-to-be) to the Torah on the Sabbath before their wedding.

Badeken: Ceremony for veiling the bride.

Erusin: Betrothal.

Get: Religious divorce, required to terminate a Jewish marriage.

Hatan: Groom.

Huppah: Wedding canopy under which bride and groom stand during wedding ceremony. May consist of a prayershawl and poles.

Kallah: Bride.

Ketubah: Marriage contract.

Kiddushin: Wedding.

Mikvah: Ritual bath.

Nesuin: Marriage.

Shadkhan: Jewish matchmaker

Sheva Berakhot: Seven wedding blessings.

Tenaim: Stipulations concerning proposed marriage.

Yihud: "Unchaperoned togetherness"; time when bride and groom are together and alone immediately following wedding ceremony.

Death and Mourning

Alav Hashalom: Hebrew for "may he rest in peace."

Aleha Hashalom: Hebrew for "may she rest in peace."

Eil Malei. Prayer for peace of departed soul.

Hevra Kaddisha: "Holy society", a group responsible for preparing the deceased for burial.

Keriah: Tearing of garment as sign of mourning.

Mourner's Kaddish: Traditional prayer affirming life, recited by mourners.

Onen: Designation of mourner prior to funeral; an onen is exempted from the performance of religious obligations.

Sheloshim: First thirty days of mourning period.

Shivah: "Seven." First seven days of mourning.

Taharah: Ritual cleansing of the deceased by the Hevra Kaddisha prior to the funeral.

Unveiling: Service marking the consecration of tombstone.

Yahrzeit: Anniversary of death, usually marked by lighting candle in memory of the deceased, saying the Mourner's Kaddish and pledging charity.

Yizkor: Memorial prayers recited on Shemini Atzeret, Passover, Shavuot and Yom Kippur.

General Terms

Ashkenazim: Jews who follow traditions of northern and central Europe.

Aveirah: Transgression of God's law.

Barukh Hashem: "May God be blessed." Expression having effect of "Thank God, I'm fine" in response to polite inquiries such as "how are you?"

Bet Din: Court of Jewish law.

Bikkur Holim: Visiting the sick, an important religious obligation.

B'nai Yisrael: "Children of Israel." The Jewish people.

Codes: Books of Jewish law.

Eretz Yisrael: The Land of Israel.

Galut: Dispersion of Jews throughout the world. Also called Diaspora.

Gemara: Major rabbinic commentary on the Mishnah, the major part of the Talmud.

Ger: A convert.

Halakha: Jewish law.

Hatikvah: "The Hope". Israel's national anthem.

Hevra: A fellowship of friends.

Hutzpah: Audacity, nerve.

Kashrut: The Jewish dietary laws.

Klezmer: Eastern European instrumental music.

Lehayim: "to Life." Toast offered before drinking wine or liquor.

Mazal tov: Expression meaning "good luck" or "congratulations."

Mentsch (Yiddish): A decent, admirable person.

Mishnah: First postbiblical code of Jewish law, elaborated upon by Gemara.

Mitzvah: A religious commandment. Judaism has 613 of them.

Naches: Joy, often from children and grandchildren.

Pushke: Tzedakah container in which coins are placed for charity.

Responsa: Formal written replies to questions on Jewish law by qualified legal authorities.

Rosh Hodesh: Beginning of new Jewish month.

Sephardim: Jews who follow traditions which originated in Spain and North Africa.

Shalom Bayit: Family harmony.

Shulchan Arukh: Authoritative Code of Jewish Law written by Joseph Karo. (sixteenth century)

Simha: Joyous occasion, often associated

with a life cycle event e.g. Bar or Bat Mitzvah or a wedding.

Talmud: Compendium of Jewish law, consisting of Mishnah and Gemara.

Tanakh: The Bible, consisting of the Torah, Prophets and Writings.

Torah: The Five Books of Moses: Genesis, Exodus, Leviticus, Numbers and Deuteronomy. Also refers to the scroll kept in the Ark from which a portion is read at worship services each week.

Tzaddik: A righteous person.

Tzedakah: Deeds of kindness. (charity)

Yarmulke (kippa in Hebrew): A skullcap.

Yom Tov: Festival

JEWISH DIETARY LAWS
IN A NUTSHELL

The Hebrew word "kosher" refers to foods that are fit to be eaten by Jewish people. All animals which chew their cud and have a split hoof are kosher. This includes cattle, sheep, goats and deer. It excludes horses, donkeys and pigs. The meat must be killed by a kosher slaughterer according to Jewish law. Once the animal has been slaughtered it must be properly salted in order to remove excess blood.

For fish to be kosher, they must have fins and scales. Thus permitted ones would include bluefish, salmon haddock, cod, flounder, halibut, herring, mackerel, pike, snapper, sardine, seabass, shad, smelt, sole, trout and tuna. Forbidden ones would include catfish, eel, shark, clam, crab, frog, lobster, octopus, oyster, scallop, shrimp and snail.

For fowl to be kosher, the birds must have a crop, an extra joint in their legs and cannot be birds of prey.

Permitted fowl would included capon, chicken, dove, duck, geese, pigeon and turkey. Forbidden fowl would include eagle, hawk, heron, ostrich, owl, pelican, and swan. Eggs from non kosher fowl are not kosher, nor are eggs with bloodspots on them.

Requirements for Kosher Kitchen: The basic requirements for a kosher kitchen are: there should be nothing non-kosher in it, and meat and dairy products and utensils need to be separated.

Permitted foods include all fresh fruits and vegetables, all unprocessed grains and cereals. All milk and most dairy products, including hard cheese, are kosher according to the Rabbinical Assembly of America, the organization of Conservative Rabbis. According to the Rabbinical Assembly of America, all machine-made wines are also kosher. This opinion is not accepted by the Orthodox Union of Rabbis.

Conservative Jews and some Reform Jews wait three or six hours after eating meat before eating dairy things. Orthodox Jews wait six hours

Kosher Symbols: Many identifying symbols have been placed on various food products identifying the product as certified kosher.

JEWISH PRAYER AND THE PRAYERBOOK IN A NUTSHELL

Before organized prayer the Israelites offered sacrifices to God, in the form of animal and meal offerings. In the ninth century of the common era, Jewish scholars in Spain appealed to Rav Amram Gaon of the Sura Academy in Babylon to supply them with a guide to the correct order of prayers. In response to this request for a definitive text of the prayer service, Rav Amram produced the first written prayerbook. This happened around 865 C.E.

Jews traditionally prayer three times daily—in the morning, afternoon and evening. The morning service is the longest in length. Following are the names of some of the major prayers in the morning daily service and their main concepts:

1. **Ma Tovu**: This is the opening prayer of the "siddur" (prayerbook). Its words "How

good are your tents O Jacob, your dwelling places O Israel" were first uttered in Numbers 24:5 by the false prophets Balaam. Balaam was originally intending to curse the Israelites, but when he saw the beauty of their tents from a hilltop, he blessed them instead. The prayer is intended to psychologically prepare the worshipper for prayer.

2. **Blessings of Morning (Birchot HaShachar)**: Consisting of 15 blessings to God, the prayer thanks God for giving the worshipper to ability to perform routine things in his or her life. (e.g. dressing oneself, getting out of bed, and so forth)

3. **Baruch She'amar**: **(Praised be God who spoke, and the world came into being)**: This prayer praises God's ability to create the world using words.

4. **Ashrei (Psalm 145: Happy are they that dwell in Your house)**: This prayer

praises God for caring for the poor and oppressed.

5. **Song of the Sea (Exodus 15)**: This prayer, taken from the Bible, is an affirmation of the Jew's belief in God's role in history. The prayer was chanted by Moses and the children of Israel after their crossing of the Red Sea.

6. **Barechu (Praised be God)**: This prayer praises God for being the Source of all blessings. Originally it was recited by the Jewish priests in the Temple as the call to worship.

7. **Shema Yisrael: Here O Israel, the Lord is our God, the Lord is One. (Deut. 6:4)**: This prayer has become the watchword of the Jewish people, proclaiming God as One God who must be loved and whose commandments must be observed.

8. **Amidah (The Standing Prayer)** This prayer, included in different forms in all worship services, blesses God for a variety of things, including giving humans knowledge, the ability to repent, healing, justice and mercy, rebuilding Jerusalem and making peace.

9. **Kaddish (Sanctification)**: There are several forms of the Kaddish prayer. In each God's name is magnified and praised.

10. **Aleinu (It is incumbent upon us to praise God)**: This prayer praises God for creating the universe and choosing the Israelites to be God's special people.

11. **Adon Olam (Eternal Sovereign)**: This prayer acknowledges that God is eternal, sovereign and redeems.

WHO'S WHO AND WHAT'S WHAT IN THE SYNAGOGUE

The synagogue as a place of congregational prayer and public instruction had come into existence long before the destruction of the second Temple in Jerusalem, over two thousand years ago. It is estimated that there were more than two thousand synagogues by the time the second Temple was destroyed in the year 70 of the common era.

During the Second Commonwealth there were hundreds of synagogues in Jerusalem and in the rural towns of ancient Israel. Throughout its long history, the synagogue has been the spiritual home of the Jew, hence the various titles by which it has been known: house of prayer, house of study, house of assembly, people's house and little sanctuary.

Jewish law contains several guidelines for the synagogue. The Holy Ark must face east, toward the holy city of Jerusalem. It is also stipulated that a synagogue must have windows. This tradition is based on the story of Daniel "in whose upper chamber he had windows made facing Jerusalem, and three times a day he knelt down, prayed and confessed to God. (Daniel 6:11)

What's in the Synagogue: Ritual Objects

1. **Bimah**: Hebrew for platform, it refers to the raised area (often appearing as a stage) from which much of the prayer service is conducted.

2. **Aron HaKodesh**: The Holy Ark, in which the Torah scrolls are placed. Generally it is located on the eastern wall of the synagogue sanctuary. A curtain is hung on the front part of the Ark with various Jewish artistic designs on it. Called the "Porochet".

3. **Torah**: Literally meaning "instruction", the Torah is the Five Books of Moses, hand written by a scribe in Hebrew by a qualified scribe. The scroll itself is attached to two wooden rollers, called "trees of life." A Torah crown, often made of silver and adorned with little bells is placed over the upper ends of the rollers.

4. **Ner Tamid**: Eternal Light, this is a lamp usually hung above the Holy Ark that glows continuously. The eternal light has often been interpreted as a symbol of the Jew, whose destiny it was to become "a light to all of the nations." (Isaiah 42:6)

5. **Amud**: This refers to the lectern from which the reading of the prayers is generally conducted.

6. **Shulchan**: The table from which the Torah is read.

7. **Menorah**: This is the candelabrum, fre-

quently used as a symbol of Judaism and the Jewish people. It has 7 lights.

8. **Yahrzeit Plaque**: These plaques, often adorning synagogue sanctuary walls, contain the names of those in the congregation who have died. Next to each name is a light which is turned on at the anniversary of the death (i.e. the yahrzeit) of the person. In addition, all of the lights of the plaque are lit at four special Memorial Services called Yizkor which take place on Passover, Shavuot, Yom Kippur and Shemini Atzeret.

Who's Who in the Synagogue

1. **Rabbi**: Meaning teacher, the rabbi is the religious and spiritual leader of the synagogue. He or she is the one to deliver the sermon as well as call the pages of the service.

2. **Cantor**: In Hebrew, the Hazzan, the can-

tor is the chanter of the liturgy and often the reader of the Torah.

3. **Gabbaim**: These people assign and call up persons for Torah honors. They also stand on either side of the "Amud" when the Torah reading is going on, to facilitate the reading and make corrections of the reader when required.

What You Need to Pray

1. **Kipa**: As a sign of reverence to God, it is customary for men (and in some synagogues women), to cover their heads while in the synagogue. In Hebrew the head covering is called a "kipa", in Yiddish it is known as a "yarmulke." The covering of the head is a sign of reverence.

2. **Tallit**: The tallit is the Hebrew word for prayershawl. Its fringes symbolize religious obligations. In Conservative synagogues, all

Jewish males (ages 13 and up) are required to wear a prayershawl. Though Jewish women are not required to wear them, they may if they choose to.

3. **Humash**: This is the Hebrew word for the Five Books of Moses, also known as the Pentateuch. It is used during the reading of the Torah to follow along. The book contains both Hebrew as well as an English translation and commentary.

4. **Siddur**: This is the prayerbook from which the liturgy is chanted. The book is both in Hebrew as well as in translation. Because Hebrew is written from right to left, the book itself opens from the right.

BLESSINGS FOR
HOME RITUAL

Judaism is primarily a home-fixed way of life. Each holiday with its home symbols, rituals, music and food can bring delight to a family. On the following pages are some of the most basic home rituals.

Blessings for Taste

Bread

בָּרוּךְ אַתָּה יְיָ, אֱלֹהֵינוּ מֶלֶךְ הָעוֹלָם,
הַמּוֹצִיא לֶחֶם מִן הָאָרֶץ.

Baruch atah Adonai eloheinu melech ha'o-lam hamotzi lechem min ha'aretz.
Praised are You, Adonai our god, Sovereign of the Universe, who brings forth bread from the earth.

Wine

בָּרוּךְ אַתָּה יְיָ, אֱלֹהֵינוּ מֶלֶךְ הָעוֹלָם, בּוֹרֵא
פְּרִי הַגָּפֶן:

Baruch ata Adonai eloheinum melech ha'o-
lam borei pri hagafen.

Praised are You, Adonai our God,
Sovereign of the Universe, who creates the
fruit of the vine.

Fruit

בָּרוּךְ אַתָּה יְיָ, אֱלֹהֵינוּ מֶלֶךְ הָעוֹלָם, בּוֹרֵא
פְּרִי הָעֵץ.

Baruch ata Adonai eloheinu melech ha'o-
lam borei pri ha'eitz.

Praised are You, Adonai our God,
Sovereign of the Universe, who creates the
fruit of the tree.

Foods that grow in the ground

בָּרוּךְ אַתָּה יְיָ, אֱלֹהֵינוּ מֶלֶךְ הָעוֹלָם, בּוֹרֵא
פְּרִי הָאֲדָמָה.

Baruch ata Adonai eloheinu melech ha'o-
lam borei pri ha-adamah.

Praised are You, Adonai our God, Sovereign of the Universe, who creates the fruit of the ground.

Blessings for Sight

Seeing a rainbow

בָּרוּךְ אַתָּה יְיָ, אֱלֹהֵינוּ מֶלֶךְ הָעוֹלָם, זוֹכֵר הַבְּרִית, וְנֶאֱמָן בִּבְרִיתוֹ, וְקַיָּם בְּמַאֲמָרוֹ.

Baruch ata Adonai eloheinu melech ha'olam zocher haberit vene'eman bivrito vekayam be'ma'amaro.

Praised are You, Adonai our God, Sovereign of the Universe, who remembers the covenant and is faithful to all promises.

Seeing lightning, shooting stars, or a sunrise.

בָּרוּךְ אַתָּה יְיָ, אֱלֹהֵינוּ מֶלֶךְ הָעוֹלָם, עוֹשֶׂה מַעֲשֵׂה בְרֵאשִׁית.

Baruch ata Adonai eloheinu melech ha'olam oseh ma'aseh bereshit.

Praised are You, Adonai our God, Sovereign of the Universe, Source of creation.

On Affixing a Mezuzah

בָּרוּךְ אַתָּה יְיָ, אֱלֹהֵינוּ מֶלֶךְ הָעוֹלָם, אֲשֶׁר קִדְּשָׁנוּ בְּמִצְוֹתָיו, וְצִוָּנוּ לִקְבֹּעַ מְזוּזָה.

Baruch ata Adonai eloheinu melech ha'o-lam asher kidshanu bemitzvotav vetzivanu likbo'ah mezuzah.

Praised are You, Adonai our God, Sovereign of the Universe, who has made us distinct with commandments and commanded us to attach the mezuzah.

On Lighting Sabbath Candles

בָּרוּךְ אַתָּה יְיָ, אֱלֹהֵינוּ מֶלֶךְ הָעוֹלָם, אֲשֶׁר קִדְּשָׁנוּ בְּמִצְוֹתָיו, וְצִוָּנוּ לְהַדְלִיק נֵר שֶׁל שַׁבָּת.

Baruch ata Adonai eloheinu melech ha'olam asher kidshanu bemitzvotav vetzivanu lehadlik ner shel Shabbat.

Praise are You, Adonai our God, Sovereign of the Universe, who has made us distinct with commandments and commanded us light the Sabbath candles.

On Lighting Candles
for a Festival

בָּרוּךְ אַתָּה יְיָ, אֱלֹהֵינוּ מֶלֶךְ הָעוֹלָם, אֲשֶׁר קִדְּשָׁנוּ בְּמִצְוֹתָיו, וְצִוָּנוּ לְהַדְלִיק נֵר שֶׁל (*on Friday:* שַׁבָּת וְ) יוֹם טוֹב.

Baruch ata Adonai eloheinu melech ha'olam asher kidshanu bemitzvotav vetzivanu lehadlik ner shel Yom Tov.

Praised are You, Adonai our God, Sovereign of the Universe, who has made us distinct with commandments and commanded us to light the festival candles.

On Lighting the Hanukkiah

בָּרוּךְ אַתָּה יְיָ, אֱלֹהֵינוּ מֶלֶךְ הָעוֹלָם, אֲשֶׁר
קִדְּשָׁנוּ בְּמִצְוֹתָיו, וְצִוָּנוּ לְהַדְלִיק נֵר
שֶׁל חֲנֻכָּה.

Baruch ata Adonai eloheinu melech ha'o-
lam asher kidshanu bemitzvotav vetzivan
lehadlik ner shel Hanukkah.

Praise are You, Adonai our God, Sovereign
of the Universe, who has made us distinct
with commandments and commanded us to
light the Hanukkah candles.

בָּרוּךְ אַתָּה יְיָ, אֱלֹהֵינוּ מֶלֶךְ הָעוֹלָם, שֶׁהֶחֱיָנוּ
וְקִיְּמָנוּ וְהִגִּיעָנוּ לִזְמַן הַזֶּה.

Baruch ata Adonai eloheinu melech ha'o-
lam she'asa nissim l'avoteynu bayamim
haheym bazman hazeh.

Praised are You, Adonai our God,
Sovereign of the Universe who has accom-
plished miracles for our ancestors from
ancient days until our time.

First Night Only:

בָּרוּךְ אַתָּה יְיָ, אֱלֹהֵינוּ מֶלֶךְ הָעוֹלָם, שֶׁהֶחֱיָנוּ וְקִיְּמָנוּ וְהִגִּיעָנוּ לִזְמַן הַזֶּה.

Baruch ata Adonai eloheinu melech ha'o-lam she-he-cheyanu vekeemanu ve-heegeeyanu lazman hazeh.

Praised are You, Adonai our God, Sovereign of the Universe for granting us life, sustaining us and enabling us to reach this day.

Blessing upon a new item, tasting a food for the first time, entering a new home, and many other new and special occasions.

בָּרוּךְ אַתָּה יְיָ, אֱלֹהֵינוּ מֶלֶךְ הָעוֹלָם, שֶׁהֶחֱיָנוּ וְקִיְּמָנוּ וְהִגִּיעָנוּ לִזְמַן הַזֶּה.

Baruch ata Adonai eloheinu melech ha'o-lam she-he-cheyanu vekeemanu ve-heegeeyanu lazman hazeh.

Praised are You, Adonai our God, Sovereign of the Universe for granting us life, sustaining us and enabling us to reach this day.

ALEF-BET

Name	Print	Script	Sound
Aleph	א	lc	silent
Bet	ב	꜒	B
(Vet)	ב	꜒	(V)
Gimel	ג	꜂	G
Dalet	ד	꜀	D
Heh	ה	꜄	H
Vav	ו	/	V
Zayin	ז	꜑	Z
Chet	ח	ᴨ	CH
Tet	ט	ꜚ	T
Yod	י	'	Y
Kaf	כּ	ꜗ	K
(Chaf)	כ	ꜗ	(CH)
(Final Chaf)	ך	ꜗ	(CH)
Lamed	ל	ʃ	L
Mem	מ	ᴎ	M
(Final Mem)	ם	ꜘ	(M)
Nun	נ	⏌	N

Name	Print	Script	Sound
Resh	ר	ר	R
Shin	שׁ	‫ׁ	SH
(Sin)	שׂ	‫	S
Tav	ת	ת	T

SINGING HATIKVAH

Kol od ba-levav pnimah
Nefesh yehudi homiyyah
U-lefa'atei mizrach kadimah
Ayin le-Tziyyon tzofiyah

Od lo avdah tikvatenu
Ha-tikvah shenot alpayim
Lihyot am chofshi be-artzenu
Eretz Tziyyon vi-Y-rushalayim.

As long as deep in the heart
The soul of a Jew years
And towards the East
An eye looks to Zion
Our hope is not yet lost
The hope of two thousand years
To be a free people in our land
The land of Zion and Jerusalem.

MOURNER'S KADDISH

The Mourner's Kaddish, a prayer recited by the bereaved in honor of his or her beloved dead, has no reference to death. Rather it is a reaffirmation of life and one's belief that God is the Supreme Judge

Yit-ga-dal ve-yit-ka-dash she-mei ra-ba, be-al-ma di-ve-ra chir-ru-tei

ve-yam-lich mal-chu-tei, be-cha-yei-chon u-ve-yo-mei-chon u-ve-chay-yei de-chol beit Yis-ra-eil, ba-a-ga-la u-vi-ze-man ka-riv ve-i-me-ru a-mein.

Ye-hei she-mei ra-ba me-va-rach le-a-lam u-le-mei al-ma-ya.

Yit-ba-rach ve-yish-ta-bach ve-yit-pa-ar ve-yit-ro-mam ve-yit-na-sei ve-yit-ha-dar ve-yit-a-leh ve-yit-ha-lal she-mei de-ku-de-sha be-rich hu, le-ei-la min kol bi-re-cha-ta ve-shi-ra-ta ,tush-be-cha-ta ve-ne-che-ma-ta, da-a-mi-ran be-al-ma ve-i-me-ru a-mein.

Ye-hei she-la-ma ra-ba min she-ma-ya, vecha-yim a-lei-nu ve-al kol yis-ra-eil, ve-i-me-ru a-mein.

O-seh sha-lom bi-me-ro-mav, hu ya-a-seh sha-lom, a-lei-nu ve-al kol yis-ra-eil, ve-i-me-ru a-mein.

Let the glory of God be extolled, let God's great name be hallowed, in the world whose creation God willed. May God's sovereignty soon prevail, in our day, our own lives, and the life of all Israel, and let us say Amen.

Let God's great name be blessed for ever and ever.

Let the name of God be glorified, exalted, and honored, though God is beyond all the praises, songs, and adorations that we can utter, and let us say Amen.

For us and for all Israel, may the blessing of peace and the promise of life come true, and let us say Amen.

May God who causes peace to reign in the high heavens, let peace descend on us, on all Israel and all the world, and let us say: Amen.

FAMOUS JEWISH QUOTATIONS

Every religion is known for famous sayings and quotations. Following is a cross section of noteworthy rabbinic sayings from Pirke Avot, the Ethics of Our Fathers:

1. The world rests on three things: on Torah, on service of God and deeds of love. (Pirke Avot 1:2)

2. If I am not for me, who will be? If I am for myself alone, what am I? If not now, when? (Pirke Avot 1:14)

3. Say little and do much. (Pirke Avot 1:15)

4. The day is short, the task is great, the workers indolent, the reward bountiful and the Master insistent. (Pirke Avot 2:20)

5. Everything is foreseen, yet freedom of choice is granted. (Pirke Avot 2:19)

6. If there is no sustenance, there is not Torah, and if there is no Torah, there is no sustenance. (Pirke Avot 2:21)

7. One good deed (i.e. mitzvah) generates another. (Pirke Avot 4:2)

8. There are three crowns: the crown of Torah, the crown of priesthood, and the crown of royalty, but the crown of a good name is superior to them all. (Pirke Avot 4:17)

9. Do not look at the flask but at its contents. (Pirke Avot 4:27)

10. One who wants to give and wants others to give, this is a saintly person. (Pirke Avot 5:15)

THE TEN COMMANDMENTS

The Ten Commandments, unequalled for simplicity and comprehensiveness, represents a summary of universal duties that are binding on all humanity. Primarily contained in Exodus 20:2–17, the Ten Commandments reappear in a somewhat modified form in Deuteronomy 5:6–21. The Ten Commandments were originally recited as part of the service in the ancient Temple in Jerusalem.

1. I am the Lord your God, who brought you out of the land of Egypt, out of the house of bondage. You shall worship only me.

2. You shall not make a graven image to worship; you shall not bow down to idols or serve them.

3. You shall not use the name of God to take a false oath.

4. Observe the Sabbath day, to keep it holy.

5. Honor your father and your mother.

6. You shall not murder.

7. You shall not commit adultery.

8. You shall not steal.

9. You shall not bear false witness against your neighbor.

10. You shall not covet your neighbor's wife, and you shall not covet your neighbor's house, or field, or servant, or anything that belongs to your neighbor.

BASIC BOOKS FOR
FURTHER READING

Garfiel, Evelyn. *Service of the Heart: A Guide to the Jewish Prayerbook*. New Jersey: Jason Aronson, 1989.

Basic Guide to understanding Jewish prayers and the prayerbook.

Glustrom, Simon *Language of Judaism*. New Jersey: Jason Aronson, 1988.

An easy-to-read book that reveals the meaning of a variety of terms and concepts vital to an understanding of Judaism.

Grayzel, Solomon. *A History of the Jews.* Philadelphia: Jewish Publication Society, 1947.

Provides a history of the Jewish people in a single volume.

Kertzer, Morris N. *What is a Jew?* New York: Macmillan Publishing, 1977.

Provides answers to more than 100 of the most commonly asked questions about Jewish life and customs.

Olitzky, Kerry M. and Isaacs, Ronald H. *A Glossary of Jewish Life*. New Jersey: Jason Aronson, 1992.
A comprehensive Jewish dictionary of words, concepts and values.

Olitzky, Kerry M. and Isaacs, Ronald H. *The How to Handbook for Jewish Living*. 3 volumes. New Jersey: Ktav Publishers, 1993, 1996, 2001.
Answers questions on how to practice Jewish customs.

Olitzky, Kerry M. and Isaacs, Ronald H. *Sacred Celebrations: A Jewish Holiday Handbook*. New Jersey: Ktav Publishers, 1994.
Provides an evocative and useful guide to both the synagogue and home family celebration of the Jewish holiday cycle.